THE HEALTHY INDOORS
new challenges
new designs

FRAM3

CONTENTS

SPACES FOR THE BODY

SPACES FOR CONNECTING

INTRODUCTION

The last decade has seen a growing interest in all aspects of health and wellbeing and designers have not been immune to this. Much of the debate has been framed in terms of providing spaces to support wellness, mindfulness as well as more established forms of medicine and healing, both through individual optimisation and self-care as well as by increasing accessibility for underrepresented groups within society. Sustainability and the use of healthy materials was another ongoing concern.

At the time of writing, the Covid-19 pandemic may still dominate the conversation, but it hasn't replaced earlier debates around wellbeing. Instead, the pandemic has acted as a catalyst for existing trends, as opposed to a new, all-encompassing reset as to what the healthy indoors might look like.

This doesn't necessarily mean that natural ventilation, easily disinfectable surfaces, home office nooks, occasional mask-wearing or individual activity pods will soon be a thing of the past. What we do see is an attempt to expand access and make these spaces more inclusive and more a part of their communities, often retrofitting existing spaces for new uses. While existing typologies may change as a result of the trend towards the sharing and experiential economies, new spatial concepts and hybrids emerge, emphasising and clustering health and wellbeing functions in places where this may not have been the case in the past.

In this publication, we've gathered 45 cutting-edge projects from 43 studios that showcase different ways in which architects and designers are approaching the creation of healthy interiors today. They are scattered all over the world and showcase the breadth of practice for designers of what we might consider to be *The Healthy Indoors*.

Divided into four chapters for easy reference, this publication seeks to catalogue these case studies not so much within strictly set types according to their brief, but instead to unravel their conceptual underpinnings. SPACES FOR WELLBEING features innovations in providing specialised and holistic medical care; while SPACES FOR PLEASURE showcases' projects which aim to delight, heal and provide peace of mind. Projects with a focus on the communal experience feature in the chapter called SPACES FOR CONNECTING; meanwhile, the SPACES FOR THE BODY chapter looks to venues dedicated to reshaping one's exterior, whether that be a nail bar, or a gym.

The architecture and design of spaces for health and wellbeing evolves constantly and we hope that readers will find *The Healthy Indoors* a useful and inspiring catalogue of solutions and concepts that they revisit and use for reference for years to come. In the meantime, we will continue our investigation of this crucial topic, both in FRAME magazine and in future publications.

SPACES FOR

WELLBEING

Below The appearance of the exterior, with its coarse facade, was designed to be crude and plain to contrast with the chaotic city.

Opposite Patients enter through a tightly closed gate where they are welcomed by a garden.

By embracing a holistic vision of medical practice, 100A ASSOCIATES' HYANGSIMJAE creates a profound connection between the physician and the patient

Jae-yoon Kim

DAEGU — Day-to-day medical care often consists of not much more than managing a patient's symptoms. Hyangsimjae clinic's proprietor, however, was looking to embody her more personal, preventative approach in the design of her workspace.

The resulting scheme, designed by Seoul-based 100A associates, is more reminiscent of a house than a typical clinic. The exterior is a minimalist composition, imbued with haptic qualities. The ground floor consists of a pared-back open kitchen and reception room, where the doctor can welcome her patients and share a light meal or perhaps a healthy drink with them before proceeding to the treatment space upstairs. The kitchen block is covered in rough-hewn stone blocks and the light-filled interior features floor-to-ceiling fenestration offering views over a series of narrow gardens that surround the buildings.

An air of easy informality permeates the space and creates the opportunity for conversations about nutrition, healthy lifestyle and preventative approaches to medicine. Upstairs, the treatment and consultation rooms are just as welcoming and informal as the kitchen downstairs. A whitewashed main space contains a traditionally laid out room with low seating for tea ceremonies, leading to an intimate, wood-panelled bathroom and spa treatment space. With an atmosphere of calm domesticity, the architects' design helps foster a more personal relationship between doctor and patient based on trust and polite conviviality.

Above The traditional Korean layout of the treatment rooms feature
low seating for tea ceremonies.

Right The whitewashed light-filled
interior gives the patient a sense of
calm domesticity.

Opposite Floor-to-ceiling fenestration offers views onto the
narrow surrounding gardens.

With an atmosphere of calm domesticity, the
architects' design helps foster a more personal
relationship between doctor and patient

The kitchen area makes the space more reminiscent of a home rather than a clinic and allows for intimacy and trust to be built between patients and specialists.

2001 combines spatial generosity, tectonic rigour and pared-back material palette in MEDIK, a polyclinic in rural Luxembourg

KAYL — Located in a small town in rural southwestern Luxembourg, the MEDIK polyclinic had to accommodate a range of medical professionals from general practitioners to opticians, dentists, paediatricians, cardiologists and physiotherapists. The building also features a cafe and a childcare facility. Faced with such a complex brief, local architecture practice 2001 took a rigorously simple approach to creating accessible, generous and naturally lit spaces integrated within a single built form.

The architect's ethos was to build 'as little as possible, but the best possible'. This resulted in a compact building with a highly regular structural grid which is carried through to MEDIK's equally regular gridded facade. The doctor–patient relationship defines the grid on which the building is designed. It liberates the interior from structural elements, enabling a myriad of design possibilities. An arcade on the ground floor gives the building a dose of metropolitan flair, while offering protection and cover to patients and medical professionals as they enter and exit. A generous, light-filled lobby with a wide stair and lifts stretches the full height of the building and allows for vertical circulation. A roof terrace is also contained within the same grid.

The interior is carried out in a similarly rational vein – the finishes are hygienic and hard-wearing but executed to a high standard. The glazed facade affords views of the surrounding countryside, a familiar and comforting sight to the users, which, like the supreme regularity of the building, is meant to reassure those seeking treatment within.

The regularity of the building's gridded facade along with the surrounding views of the countryside provides a sense of comfort to the medical center's patients.

Views of the lush post-industrial landscape and the regularity of the building are meant to comfort and reassure those seeking treatment within

The architect's ethos was to build 'as little as possible, but the best possible'

Above The secretaries have a view of the wide stairways and lifts that stretch along the full height of the building.

Opposite The interior features high-standard, hygienic and hard-wearing finishes.

A+R ARCHITEKTEN combines local, low-cost materials and techniques with a robust, simple layout in PROJECT BURMA HOSPITAL

Oliver Gerhartz

Shading folding shutters on the windows and woven bamboo mats covering the ceilings favour optimal air circulation and a pleasant draught all throughout the building.

MAGYIZIN — Healthcare might be a universal human right, but providing suitable facilities in remote regions of the world can be challenging. Located on Myanmar's west coast, a region virtually inaccessible during the rainy season, and financed by the German charity Projekt Burma e.V., a+r Architekten's Project Burma Hospital is humane architecture at its best.

The hospital is built around a central courtyard, which doubles as a waiting room. Being open to the elements helps to limit the transmission of diseases, while deep eaves shelter the building and its users from the sun and rain. In order to keep costs low, the architects have used building methods local to the region. This also made it possible to construct the building using local labourers and ensures its future maintenance is achievable. A sturdy concrete frame is filled in with red bricks and timber windows and screens. A tropical roof with a bamboo mat ceiling enables natural cooling and cross-ventilation.

The main quadrangle hosts consultation rooms and even the region's first surgical operating theatre. A linear block to the side accommodates further individual wards, with communal facilities and storage spaces. As the new hospital is situated on higher ground, it also doubles as an emergency shelter during flash floods and tsunamis. By adapting the hospital typology to the building's context, the architects have designed a crucial piece of health infrastructure to serve the local community.

The hospital was designed according to the country's typical 'brick nogging structure', with a skeleton made of reinforced concrete and brick filling.

The new hospital is situated on higher ground and doubles as an emergency shelter during flash floods and tsunamis

Below Consultation rooms are located within the main quadrangle of the building.

Opposite Stones from the local beach, collected by the villagers, line the central basin of the inner courtyard and serve as a water drain.

ARHITEKT MUST's SUURE-JAANI HEALTH CENTRE

combines small-town scale with generous health, leisure and civic facilities

Above **Historic rubble and the area's characteristic red brick is maintained and displayed throughout the centre.**

Opposite **The six-volumed complex, adjoining a historical fire station tower, preserves the small-town scale of the surrounding village.**

Suure-Jaani Health Centre by Arhitekt Must

SUURE-JAANI — Trying to combat central Estonia's rural depopulation, Arhitekt Must's new scheme provides locals with a plethora of facilities, including a cafe, health centre, rehabilitation clinic, swimming pool, sauna, ambulance, police and tourist information centre. At the same time, the architect wished to cautiously preserve the small-town scale so characteristic of the area.

Built next to an existing fire station tower, the programme is divided into six smaller, two-storey volumes. Featuring pitched roofs and covered in red brick, the external massing of the new centre is in keeping with the form and the scale of the surrounding village. The void between the volumes is covered, accommodating a swimming pool and a spa. Inspired by the region's Sooma National Park's annual floods, the pool recreates the atmosphere of high water as the pools come close to the edge of the 'houses' that comprise the complex. A rectangular pool morphs into a shallow, organically shaped paddling pool for children, while a jacuzzi and a water slide are off to the side, providing uninterrupted views of the countryside. Expanses of grey floor tiles and white ceiling create an open feeling throughout the space. The wellness centre, containing a sauna and spa facilities, is located within one of the volumes and is covered in smaller brown ceramic tiles and pale wood, creating a more sheltered, intimate atmosphere.

The wellness centre is lined with pale wood to create a sheltered, intimate atmosphere.

The pools are designed as a flooded field of water, mimicking the boglands of the surrounding area.

Suure-Jaani Health Centre by Arhitekt Must

Spaces for Wellbeing

The central void between the buildings hosts a water park, swimming pool and spa, reminiscent of the nearby Sooma National Park's floods.

Suure-Jaani Health Centre by Arhitekt Must

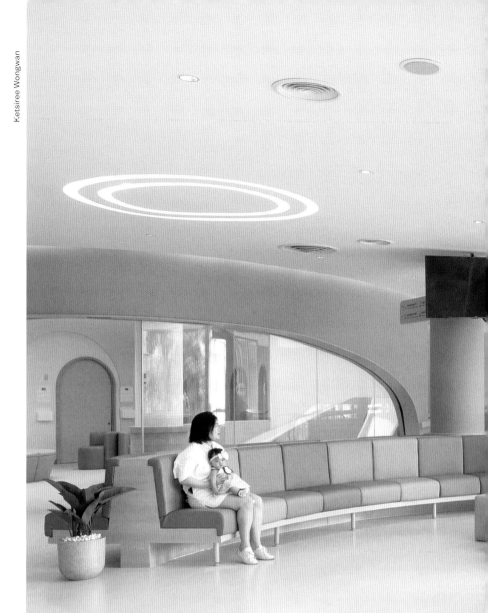

INTEGRATED FIELD
brings curves, pastel
colours and a sense
of fun into EKACHAI
HOSPITAL for children

Colours, shapes and curved lines relate to the children, while the slide leading from the second to the first floor engages the children's natural desire for play.

SAMUT SAKHON — A visit to the hospital is rarely a pleasant experience, but it could always be less unpleasant. It could even be, whisper it, a little bit fun. At Ekachai Children's Hospital on the southwestern edge of Bangkok, local studio Integrated Field tried making the experience more palatable by channelling the interior architects' inner child, bringing colour, curves and special decorative features to ease anxiety among its patients as well as their parents and guardians.

The fun starts at the avocado-green entrance – two escalators take children up to the waiting area. To the side, a bright yellow slide stands waiting to take the jubilant patients back down and out. The waiting room consists of curving seating and freestanding, cubic ottomans. From there, curving corridors lead to individual wards, each of which has a dedicated colour scheme – think warm, cotton-candy and pastels. Arched doorways and gently backlit walls throughout complete this soft image. The hospital also includes a round, sky-blue swimming pool with cut-out clouds adorning the upper portions of the walls and the ceiling.

The patients' rooms are designed to be just as soothing, with timber flooring and stellar-constellation-themed artwork on the walls doubling as luminaires. Throughout the design, the architects have managed to appeal to children's whimsical sensibilities as well as providing them with a bright, diverting space in which to heal.

Each room in the hospital features a constellation on the ceiling, respecting the room's theme animal, serving as a comforting companion and a night light.

The waiting rooms are designed
as playgrounds, a space where
children can play.

Throughout the design, the interior architects have managed to appeal to children's whimsical sensibilities

KAUNITZ YEUNG ARCHITECTURE's PUNTUKURNU AMS HEALTHCARE HUB
uses the ancient building technique to create a connection with the land on which it stands

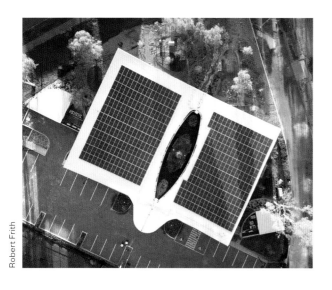

Robert Frith

Below The roof from both wings of the building slopes towards the central courtyard, the heart of the hub.

Opposite A large photovoltaic system on the roof allows the centre to be powered by nearly 100 per cent solar energy.

Puntukurnu AMS Healthcare Hub by Kaunitz Yeung Architecture

NEWMAN — When designing a new health clinic for the Aboriginal community in Western Australia, architecture studio Kaunitz Yeung Architecture has sought to create a building that would be connected with the land and the people it serves. After all, this was to be the first primary care centre to be built in the area.

By adopting an extensive co-design process, the architects were able to work together with the community to develop a design which would address both their practical and cultural needs. A sheltered courtyard with mature eucalyptus trees forms the heart of the project and doubles as a waiting room and an occasional event space. A series of rammed earth pavilions are open to this green space and together the two are united by a vast sweeping roof above as well as a timber deck underfoot.

Locally-sourced rammed earth creates a strong connection to the surrounding landscape, but its bulk also protects the inside of the health hub from the scorching heat. The whitewashed interiors feature tall, narrow windows, letting in just enough light, but protecting the interior from overheating. Specially made metal screens, designed by 19 Aboriginal artists from the surrounding area, protect the patients' privacy, filter out the light and secure the courtyards when the clinic is closed.

A sheltered courtyard with mature eucalyptus trees forms the heart of the project and doubles as a waiting room

Right **Artwork featured throughout the building originates from five local indigenous communities.**

Opposite **Downpour from the roof is naturally directed towards the courtyard, sustainably and passively watering the eucalyptus trees.**

Walls made of locally-sourced rammed earth create a strong connection to the environment and to the area's aboriginal community.

Puntukurnu AMS Healthcare Hub by Kaunitz Yeung Architecture

LACROIX CHESSEX-designed MEDICO-SOCIAL SUPPORT STRUCTURE FOR ELDERLY PEOPLE features a low profile and a prefabricated facade

ECHICHENS — The new Medico-social support structure for elderly people serves as a short-stay facility for patients who do not need full hospital care during their recovery, but who nevertheless benefit from specialised attention, care and monitoring before being discharged. The design by Geneva-based architecture studio Lacroix Chessex is more inspired by hospitality than by hospitals. As such, the scheme includes a hair salon and a tea-room, alongside a doctor's practice and other medical facilities.

The restrained, two-storey built volume is arranged around two patios, with individual rooms facing outward. Large floor-to-ceiling windows frame views of the surrounding countryside and village church. The structure and facade of the building are made using pale prefabricated concrete elements, giving the low-slung complex a sense of robustness and regularity. Dual, planted patios offer more sheltered, communal spaces.

Inside, the pared-back material and colour palette of the exterior continues. The lobbies and corridors are covered in polished concrete, with maroon skirting boards, doors and window frames, while whitewashed walls and timber floors in the individual rooms create a calm atmosphere throughout. The second-storey spaces also feature exposed concrete rafters and timber ceilings as a nod to the region's vernacular architecture. The building exudes a sense of restraint and tranquillity to aid patients with their recovery while providing a sense of normalcy to those leaving medical care.

The building offers views of the surrounding country- side and the village church

Olivier di Giambattista

Medico-social support structure for elderly people by Lacroix Chessex   43

The structure and facade of the building is made using pale prefabricated concrete elements

Above **Planted patios offer sheltered, communal spaces.**

Opposite **Pale prefabricated concrete elements make up the building's facade, giving it a sense of regularity.**

Above **Hospitality-focused, the centre
features a tea-room offering patients
a comforting space to recover.**

Opposite **The timeless design gives
patients a sense of familiarity and
regularity**

The design by Geneva-based architecture studio Lacroix Chessex is more inspired by hospitality than by hospitals

NATASHA THORPE DESIGN's scheme for GO ORTHODONTISTES DOWNTOWN FLAGSHIP brings a welcome dose of golden glamour to the world of dentistry

MONTREAL — It might seem like the interior of the new Go Orthodontistes Downtown Flagship takes its cue from the name of the Golden Square Mile neighbourhood in which it stands. However, the scheme's golden sheen, courtesy of local studio Natasha Thorpe Design, is a glamorous alternative to the usual, 'anxiety-inducing' feel of medical spaces.

Combining various materials and textures, such as gold-coloured, metal mesh curtains and ceiling panels, honey-coloured marble tiles, a warm limestone reception desk, as well as a red brick and stainless-steel communal sink, the design brings an unexpected touch of luxury to what are often functional spaces. At the same time, Corian cabinets in the communal treatment room and a polished concrete floor throughout ensure practicality, hygiene and easy maintenance. Even the gold-coloured curtains double as privacy screens between the dental chairs. A conference room and toilet block are concealed within a white corrugated steel element towards the back of the space. Small, golden bleachers at the entrance double as a waiting area and add a touch of whimsy.

Taken together, the scheme creates a visually rich and harmonious environment, which is kept consistent by a singular golden colour palette. At the same time, the studio's attention to detail and function ensures that patients receive the highest level of care.

Maxime Brouillet

The light-catching colour
scheme of the office accentu-
ates natural daylight flooding
the clinic.

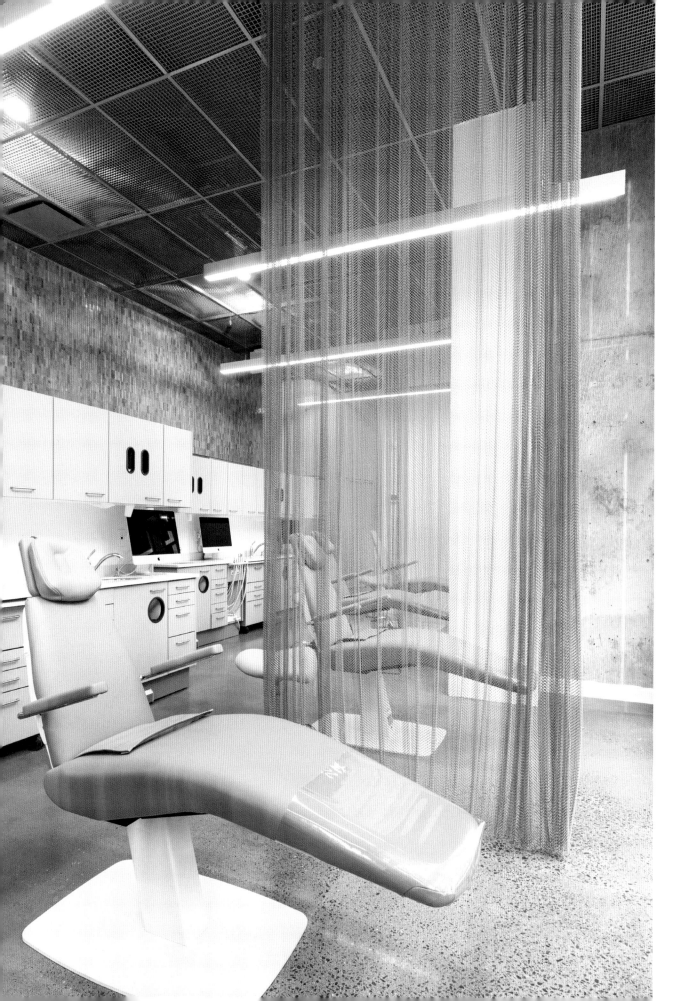

This page **Small golden bleachers in the entrance double as a waiting area.**

Opposite **Gold-coloured, metal mesh curtains serve as dividers between patients, while offering a luxurious touch to the dental clinic.**

The scheme's golden sheen is a glamorous alternative to the usual, 'anxiety-inducing' connotation of a medical space

Left Corrugated white steel conceals a conference room and staff office, while catching patients' eyes with its texture and curved form.

Below Gold mesh panels lining the ceiling plunge the space in a warm, golden hue.

Go Orthodontistes Downtown Flagship by Natasha Thorpe Design

CBD, the other active chemical in hemp on sale at STANDARD DOSE, gets a high-end wellness rebrand, courtesy of SR PROJECTS AND TUNA

Left Rough plastering, topped with a soft peach colour was utilized to establish a pervasive feeling of calm and emphasise texture and touch.

Below Tiles in a soft pink palette add another layer of texture to the area, while still being in harmony with the soft space.

David Mitchell

NEW YORK — CBD, the other active ingredient derived from hemp, is known for its medicinal properties. Like THC, it can be used to relieve pain and anxiety, but it is not psychoactive and is less stringently regulated. However, the association with stoner culture lingers and designers, entrepreneurs and architects are busy trying to recast CBD in a wellness mould.

Enter architecture studios SR Projects and TUNA as well as CDB brand Standard Dose, whose Manhattan store was designed with the image of wellness at the forefront. Located in a typically narrow and tall retail unit, the architects have opted for a minimalist, but nevertheless inviting scheme. Peach-coloured walls with built-in display shelves – roughly rendered on one side and tiled on the other – define the space, while a bright white ceiling with louvres perpendicular to the walls creates a sense of lightness. A terrazzo countertop adds a touch of contemporary luxury that Standard Dose wanted for the project.

The idea of wellness and wellbeing is bolstered even further by a meditation room at the back of the store. Here, customers are encouraged to try the various products, such as CBD infused food and drinks, oils and cosmetics. With low informal seating arranged under an artificial skylight, Standard Dose reinvents CBD as part of a healthy, aspirational lifestyle.

Located in a typically narrow and tall retail space, the architects have opted for minimalist, but inviting atmosphere

Low seating, soft arched openings, a manicured jade plant and an artificial skylight set the sense of wellness in the meditation room.

A radiused corner and large
yucca plant provide customers
with a sense of comfort, lightness, life and warmth.

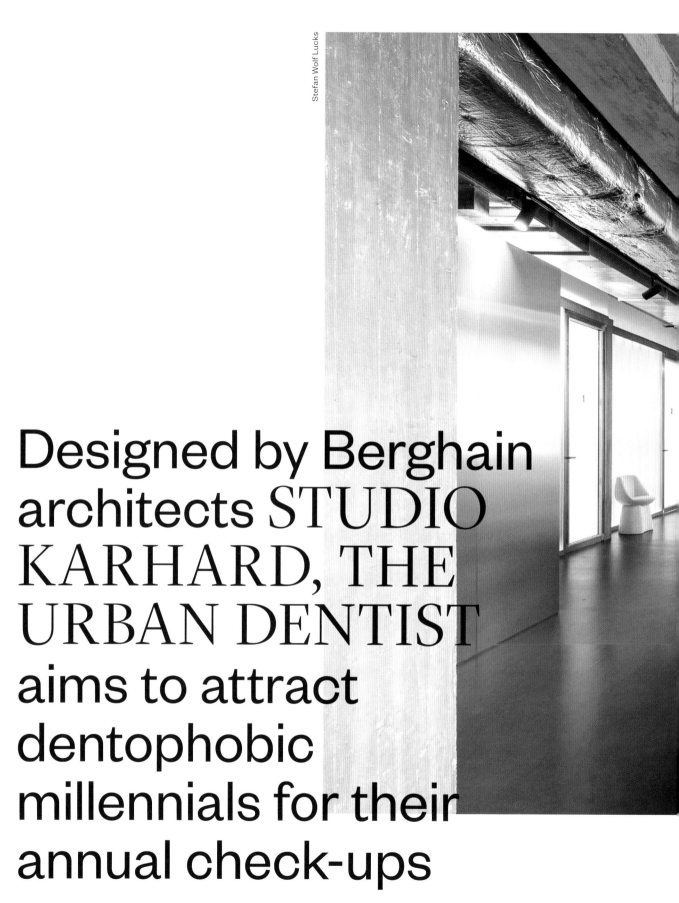

Designed by Berghain architects STUDIO KARHARD, THE URBAN DENTIST aims to attract dentophobic millennials for their annual check-ups

Colourful upholstered seating
and a backlit glass wall make up
the clinic's waiting area.

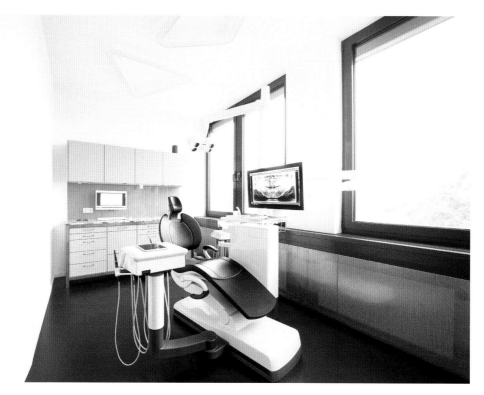

Above The centre's bold theme is maintained within the individual treatment rooms with their bright pink cabinets and brass accents contrasting the dark linoleum floor.

Opposite The dark terrazzo reception desk and orange tinted mirrors uphold the clinic's daring theme, while exposed concrete ceilings and air ducts recall Berlin's industrial inspired nightclubs.

BERLIN — Going to the dentist's office is never a pleasant experience and in Germany, people aged 25 to 34 lagged behind other age groups by six to seven per cent in visiting a dental clinic, according to a 2014 Eurostat survey. Undeterred, three young dentists based in Europe's party capital decided that the best way to encourage their peers was to engage studio karhard, the designers of the legendary Berghain nightclub.

'They wanted to make the patients feel comfortable and fearless,' says studio's co-founder Thomas Karsten. Eschewing the clinical, all-white aesthetic, the space feels more like a concept store or a bar than somewhere to get a root canal. The architects' choices of materials and furnishings –

black linoleum floor, a blocky terrazzo reception desk and dusky pink upholstered seating in the waiting room – fully support the design intent. Orange tinted mirrors behind the reception add to the bold colour palette, but also conceal the more mundane offices located behind them.

Exposed concrete columns, ceilings and air-ducts are reminiscent of Berlin's industrial inspired nightclubs, as are the U-channel glass walls with integrated programmable lighting. Even the cabinets within the individual treatment rooms have received a glamorous makeover with brass accents and pastel colours. Visiting the dentist may never be a party, but this is as close as it gets.

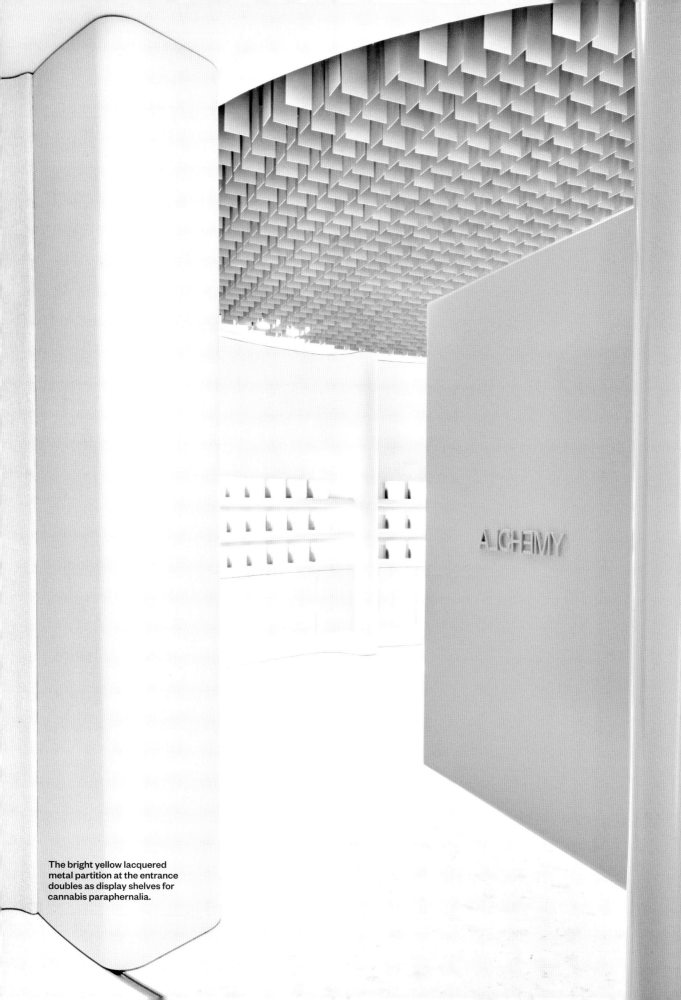

The bright yellow lacquered metal partition at the entrance doubles as display shelves for cannabis paraphernalia.

ALCHEMY

Joel Esposito

STUDIO PAOLO FERRARI takes cannabis from the backstreet to the high street in the new minimalist dispensary ALCHEMY

TORONTO — Dubbed 'Canada's first immersive cannabis retail store' by the designer Paolo Ferrari, Alchemy is a masterclass in carefully curated spatial experience. A tree breaking through the terrazzo floor in the entrance hall greets customers and embodies the tension between the organic and the technical. The studio describes this juxtaposition as falling somewhere between 'a laboratory and a temple', rejecting cannabis clichés by fusing art, nature and technology to deliver 'a cerebral experience'.

Inside the white main circular chamber, a bright yellow lacquered metal shelf displays cannabis accessories while white Corian shelves along the curving perimeter showcase the minimally packaged products. Reminiscent of an apothecary, edibles are laid out in a dedicated area of specially created belljar pods. An organically formed niche – made of red-orange eco-resin – creates another opportunity to display bongs, pipes and other accessories.

While saturated colour is used to highlight product displays in the main space, the check-out room defaults back to neutral pale unglazed terracotta tiles and features a rectangular counter made of the same material. The project's collage of materials and accent colours highlighting distinct experiential zones stimulates curiosity about the products, while the pared-back background highlights Alchemy's position as a holistic and healthful lifestyle brand.

Left The main circular perimeter is lined by white Corian shelves to showcase the minimally packaged products.

Below Red-orange eco-resin makes up an organically formed niche, fostering the sense of curiosity and discovery.

Opposite Neutral, unglazed terra-cotta tiles ground clients as they check-out from the minimalist dispensary.

Alchemy's interior rejects cannabis clichés by fusing art, nature and technology to deliver 'a cerebral experience'

Bright pops of colour are used to highlight product displays, while the pared-back background reflects the store's position on holistic health.

Alchemy by Studio Paolo Ferrari

Combining accessible patient facilities with cutting-edge labs, WIEGERINCK's AMSTERDAM UMC IMAGING CENTER hopes to improve the effectiveness of cancer treatment

William Moore

Right **A close-up of the window frames' detailing.**

Opposite **The building's circulation is placed against its extensively glazed facade.**

Hanne van der Woude

Above **Sophisticated medical equipment can be glimpsed along either side of the atrium.**

Opposite **The entrance leads to a light-filled atrium, the 'lungs' of the building, flanked by individual consultation rooms.**

AMSTERDAM — Advances in medical imaging, including sophisticated MRI and CT scans, hold great promise in helping usher in a new era of personalised medicine, where doctors can tailor potential treatments to their patients' individual needs. In the Dutch capital, studio Wiegerinck was faced with a challenging task: to design a space where patients feel at ease, while doctors and medical researchers can run sophisticated diagnostics and create the essential isotopes used in radiotherapy.

The Amsterdam UMC Imaging Center, located at one of the city's largest hospitals, comprises a compact, fully glazed volume, with its own entrance, reached via a generous arcade. Leading to a light filled atrium flanked by individual consultation rooms, the generous, yet compact entrance sequence helps put patients at ease, while ensuring that seriously ill people never have to walk too far. At the same time, sophisticated medical equipment can be glimpsed along either side, giving visitors reassuring insight into the workings of the cutting-edge lab.

Similarly, placing the building's circulation against the extensively glazed facade creates a transparent, approachable building, while allowing researchers and medics who spend much of their days in artificially lit laboratories to get a glimpse of the outside. The UMC Imaging Center provides a welcome contrast to the conventional, inward looking medical buildings that surround it.

Above The centre was designed
for the comfort of patients, visitors
and staff.

Opposite Curved corners in the
corridors provide a sense of safety
and security.

The studio designed a space
where patients feel at ease
while researchers can run
sophisticated diagnostics

The laser lab and tracer centre
on the top floors can be seen
through the building's atrium.

Built in just four days, ST. CAROLUS HOSPITAL SCREENING FACILITY designed by AT-LARS shows how quick-thinking architects can react to a public health emergency

JAKARTA — The Covid-19 pandemic saw architects and designers creating makeshift hospitals, developing more efficient ventilators or even 3D printing components to provide face shields for medical staff. In Jakarta, AT-LARS has created a Covid screening facility in front of the entrance of the city's St. Carolus Hospital, in order to prevent infecting vulnerable patients inside. The architects have inserted the structure underneath a canopy located at the edge of the hospital car park, connecting it to the natural flow of people entering the building. Straddling a planted border, the screening facility is nestled comfortably within its site.

The semi-permanent, 32-m-long, 140-m^2 pavilion was erected in just four days using scaffolding tubes, hardwood floor, polycarbonate wall panels and a corrugated uPVC roof. Large gaps between the components enable natural ventilation, which helps to disperse any pathogens. The translucent materials create a subtle visual connection between inside and outside, ensuring visitors are able to see the movement of people within, while also helping to reduce energy consumption during the day.

Flexible, extendable and demountable, AT-LARS' structure at Jakarta's St. Carolus Hospital demonstrates how architects and designers can respond to an emergency and adapt simple, off-the-shelf materials and components to suit a particular context and function.

The structure is inserted comfortably underneath a canopy at the edge of the hospital car park.

William Sutanto

St. Carolus Hospital Screening Facility by AT-LARS

Below Partition walls separate each waiting cubicle, as well as the facility's major areas.

Bottom Large gaps between the components enable natural and cross-ventilation.

Left The facility features scaffolding tubes, bangkirai wooden flooring, polycarbonate wall panels and a corrugated uPVC roof.

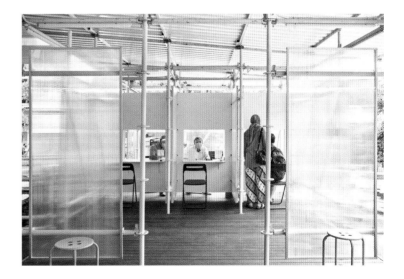

St. Carolus Hospital Screening Facility by AT-LARS

Large gaps in the structure enable natural ventilation, which helps to disperse any pathogens

Above **A planted border lines the screening facility.**

Opposite **Translucent cladding creates a subtle visual connection between inside and outside.**

KEY TAKEAWAYS

1. UNDERSTANDING AND ANTICIPATING the clients' and users' needs and wishes and the type of INTERPERSONAL CONNECTION they are aiming for can help in creating appropriately functional, but also decorative and artistic solutions to a project.

2. Refurbishing existing spaces, drawing on familiar spatial typologies as well as using local materials and iconography can create spaces with a STRONG LOCAL IDENTITY and SENSE OF CONNECTION.

3. It is paramount that any design fosters A SENSE OF COMMUNITY AND UTILITY – not only between the scheme's immediate users, but also implicitly serving the wider network of the city, town or village.

4. Designers need to focus on creating A FEELING OF SAFETY AND INCLUSIVITY in the broadest sense. The most successful projects create truly popular and accessible platforms for communal life, whether for specific activities, relaxation or other functions.

SPACES FOR

PLEASURE

By removing clutter, furniture and even walls, ALAN PREKOP's minimalist FLAT IO gives its owner a peace of mind

BRATISLAVA — For enthusiastic adopters, minimalism – letting go of unnecessary possessions and simplifying one's life – is a sure path to a stress-free, happy existence. Reworking an old, somewhat poky flat in the oldest purpose-built housing estate in the Slovak capital, architect Alan Prekop decided that what the space needed was a radical minimalist makeover.

Prekop has thoroughly decluttered the flat, removing most dividing walls and abolishing the dark internal corridors, allowing the space to be replanned according to the occupier's desire for simplicity. Only a single load-bearing column (the 'I'), located in the centre of the flat, stayed.

A generous kitchen is divided from the living space by a wall featuring a large, circular opening lined with stainless steel (the 'O').

While the concrete ceilings and beams are exposed, the perimeter walls have a fresh layer of plaster and white tiles cover the lower part of the wall. The bedroom is accessed using glass doors, with a curtain giving additional privacy and open shelves highlighting the owner's preference for mindful, clean living. The restrained minimalism of the interior is not just skin deep; much of the material used in the renovation originates from building waste generated elsewhere in the city.

Nora&Jakub

The 'O': a large circular opening lined with stainless steel creates an open division between the kitchen and living space.

Flat IO by Alan Prekop

Much of the material
used in the renovation
originates from building
waste generated
elsewhere in the city

Above A wooden partition and
curtains provide the bedroom
with privacy while maintaining
the space's open concept.

Right The doors to the bathroom
and toilet are concealed within the
galvanised sheet metal, creating
the feeling of a single unit.

Opposite Concrete ceilings and
exposed beams, contrasted with
white plastered walls and ceramic
tiles embody the minimalistic concept of the flat.

ATELIER CARACAS-designed FUN MAZE! and 2020: A SPA ODYSSEY both share a surrealist streak

CARACAS — Despite two very different briefs, Atelier Caracas takes the same surrealist approach for these two spaces in the Venezuelan capital, the waiting room of a multidisciplinary therapy centre for children and a day spa. In both instances, the aim is to subvert the everyday and put people at ease, be they patients and their parents or spa-goers.

At the Fun Maze!, the architects have created a colourful, haptic space to facilitate educational therapy for children on the spectrum. A corridor, defined by curving, roughly plastered turquoise walls, leads to treatment rooms on either side. A linear skylight running the length of the building floods the space with natural light, while domed porthole windows – at children's eye-level – offer views through the clinic and glimpses of the large potted plants that are dotted across the space. Playful nooks and crannies along the corridor can be used to hide toys, fostering a sense of discovery throughout.

At 2020: A Spa Odyssey, the architects were inspired by the surreal visuals in the classic *2001: A Space Odyssey*. They have integrated some of the film's unmistakable sci-fi stylings, such as round window openings and rounded corners on the partitions that separate the individual treatment rooms, high gloss floors and even a meteoroid supporting the reception desk. Once again, large houseplants make an appearance, domesticating the space and helping reinforce the illusion of the spa as a 'pleasant, hermetic bubble'.

Saúl Yuncoxar

Domed porthole windows
at children's eye level offer
views throughout the clinic.

Right The triangular roof, made of galvanized sheeting and glass, floods the centre with natural light.

Opposite Roughly plastered curving turquoise walls give the impression of a ludic and friendly labyrinth.

Nooks and crannies along the corridor can be used to hide toys, fostering a sense of discovery throughout

Circular windows, rose tinted glass separations and sci-fi designs are reminiscent of Kubrick's iconic *2001: A Space Odyssey.*

Architects were inspired by the surreal visuals in the sci-fi classic *2001: A Space Odyssey*

Above **The centre's otherworldly details elevate the space to an experience.**

Right **Pastel pink walls and ground-sourced materials remind us of home as a contrast to the outer space interior.**

Opposite **High gloss floors, rounded partition walls and a 'meteoroid' supporting the front desk submerge spa-goers in the surreal.**

CARLOS ZWICK ARCHITEKTEN BDA's HAUS AM SEE

combines expansive views, lakeside setting and environmental concerns

POTSDAM — Located on a wooded lakeside plot not far from the German capital, Carlos Zwick Architekten BDA's design for Haus am See addresses multiple constraints. Some were imposed by the authorities – the terraced site, once a beloved respite of the Kaiser himself, had to be preserved, along with the views of the water from the main road. Others, such as the desire to keep the mature trees, or to incorporate sweeping views of the water, were self-imposed by the architect, who lives in the house with his wife and their six children.

Raising the house on triangular stilts means that the views through the site have been preserved. Two volumes – one at the water's edge containing the living areas and a smaller volume at the back containing the bedrooms – have been arranged around one of the old trees. In fact, the tree stands in the middle of the house, creating a small patio and the feeling of living in a treehouse.

A wide terrace runs the entire length of the raised volume eight metres above the water level, opening views of the surrounding nature. The exterior of the home is clad in larch planks, emphasising the connection to nature. Inside, the bright and generous open-plan living areas create a flexible setting for a large family. Built using natural, recyclable materials such as steel, wood and cellulose fibre, the structure is also built to a Passive House standard, which helps ensure a comfortable indoor climate while also significantly lowering energy consumption.

Below **Vertical larch wood slats make up the structure's facades.**

Opposite **The lakeside property, surrounded with ancient trees, stands on 40 diagonal iron stilts, only touching the terrace below at specific points.**

José Campos

Haus am See by Carlos Zwick Architekten BDA

Sliding floor-to-ceiling wooden windows allow for extreme proximity to the surrounding natural environment.

Above A fireplace within the
home creates a sense of comfort
and warmth.

Right A long olive wood dining
table and warm colours recall
the home's connection to nature.

Spaces for Pleasure

The structure is also built to a Passive House standard, helping ensure a comfortable indoor climate while also significantly lowering energy consumption

Haus am See by Carlos Zwick Architekten BDA

A wide terrace runs the entire length
of the raised volume eight metres
above the water level, opening views
of the surrounding nature

Below **Relaxing on the wide terrace gives the impression of floating directly on the lake's surface.**

Opposite **The natural flow of the
house's layout fosters a peaceful
environment.**

Wood grains and natural fibres create tactile connections to nature throughout the office, coupled with multiple large, oxygenating indoor plants.

Taking a holistic view of employee health and wellbeing, COOKFOX-designed INTERNATIONAL WELL BUILDING INSTITUTE leads by example

NEW YORK — WELL is the first holistic, global set of standards dedicated to healthy buildings in the broadest sense, with seven categories – air, water, nourishment, light, fitness, comfort and mind – encompassing both spatial and building fabric strategies that improve user wellbeing. When it came to designing the new WELL Building Institute in an existing 1912 building overlooking Manhattan's Madison Square Park, COOKFOX Architects took it as a challenge to prove that older structures could be retrofitted to the same high standard of wellbeing as new builds.

Featuring whitewashed walls and exposed ceilings, the light-filled, airy space uses sustainable, low emission materials, eliminating as many volatile organic compounds as possible. An advanced air filtration system, coupled with large amounts of oxygenating indoor plants ensures high quality indoor air. A spacious, well-stocked employee kitchen encourages interaction and healthy nutrition, while a large breakout space in the corner of the building features a low-slung sofa which offers expansive views of the surrounding cityscape.

An array of adjustable employee desks, including standing desks with stationary bicycles and balance boards encourage healthy habits within the workspace, while bicycle storage encourages active commuting. Further policies, such as the possibility of remote working, help promote employee wellbeing. Taken together, these design moves enabled the office of the certification institute to be awarded a WELL Platinum certification.

Below Whitewashed walls and
exposed ceilings create an airy
atmosphere.

Opposite The space's carpeting
features a biomimetic pattern
which was inspired by lichen.

Adjustable employee desks, including
standing desks with stationary bicycles
and balance boards encourage healthy
habits within the workspace

Exposed original brick walls and patinaed brass window frames help preserve the building's historical context and add unique texture.

GG-LOOP
combines biophilia with parametricism, resulting in FREEBOOTER duplexes full of light, air and space

AMSTERDAM — Located on a corner lot in the Dutch capital's newly built Zeeburgereiland district, studio GG-loop combined the power of parametric design with biophilic principles to create Freebooter. This pair of stacked homes takes its name from the country's maritime explorers, in an ode to the views of the water apparent throughout. At the same time, the architects were committed to the inhabitants' wellbeing, creating two airy homes made using natural materials and organic, curving geometry.

The house's facade is fully glazed to maximise views out, while cantilevered terraces and timber louvres – the dimensions of which were determined parametrically by the sun's path across the sky – form a screen along the building's perimeter. These help counter overheating during the summer months and ensure privacy for the inhabitants. The curving forms of the facade are also reflected in the interior's rounded corners, allowing a natural flow of movement throughout the house.

Using renewable cross-laminated timber enabled off-site prefabrication, ensuring that the building has a minimal ecological footprint. In addition to naturally regulating humidity, wooden surfaces have been found to reduce stress levels in humans, which alongside the homes' sweeping views help ensure residents feel a sense of calm and wellbeing. Taken together, GG-loop's residential project updates the modernist mantra of 'light, air and space' to provide calm amidst 21st century life.

Timber louvres along the house's facade were designed parametrically using the sun's path, ensuring privacy and countering overheating within the apartments.

Michael Sieber

Freebooter by GG-loop

Michael Sieber

Above **Cantilevered terraces provide the dwellers with sweeping views and a sense of calm.**

Opposite **Optimal sunlight floods the apartments.**

Spaces for Pleasure

Francisco Nogueira

Right The project, inspired by maritime constructions, features western red cedar, pine and steel: materials highly used in building ships and requiring strong timberwork.

Below The flow of spaces and organic lines, designed with the dwellers in mind, provides a healthy space for rest and living.

Michael Sieber

Spaces for Pleasure

In addition to naturally regulating humidity, wooden surfaces have been found to reduce stress levels in humans

The pods, elevated so as to not
disturb the surrounding, offer a
full immersion into the Swiss alps.

Spaces for Pleasure

Creating a connection with nature is paramount to MONTALBA ARCHITECTS, whether in WHITEPOD, ZEN SUITE eco-resort or their VERTICAL COURTYARD HOUSE

Delphine Burtin

SANTA MONICA, MONTHEY — Based in both California and Switzerland, Montalba Architects might work across two different continents, but the practice's work is always underpinned by the desire to bring users closer to nature.

The studio's Zen Suite at the Whitepod eco-resort features expansive views of an Alpine valley in Switzerland and consists of a series of geodesic domes with a bathroom segment at the back. The minimalist design is guided by the concept of Zen and by Wu Ting movement theory which stresses the connected nature of material, form and energy. The circular main space contains a sunken rounded segment with 'tatami' floor and a bed with a view out over the valley, while the back of the pod is clad in timber and contains a connected chamber with a circular bath.

At the Vertical Courtyard House, the architects have created an airy three-storey residence located in the iconic Santa Monica Canyon. Featuring a central atrium and timber louvres, the interior can be fully naturally ventilated. Floor-to-ceiling windows and the use of pale wood and concrete in both the interior and exterior courtyard create a seamless link between the inside and the outside. Designed in conjunction with a small, sheltered garden, the house becomes a part of the landscape that can be effortlessly inhabited in a number of different ways.

Left Views of the mountains can be seen from within the structures.

Opposite The curved wooden walls of the pod bring attention to the bed – the space's focal point – while maintaining harmony with the natural landscapes.

Montalba Architects' work is always underpinned by the desire to bring users closer to nature

Floor-to-ceiling windows
and use of pale wood and
concrete in both interiors
create a seamless link
between the inside and
the outside

Below Various natural materials were used in the design of the home and chosen based on criteria of light reflectivity, texture and durability.

Opposite A series of operable glass doors, mobile louvered shades and overhanging balconies provides the home with both privacy and circulation, while preventing overheating during summer months.

Whitepod, Zen Suite and Vertical Courtyard House by Montalba Architects

Above The openness of the home
allows for all three floors, including
the basement, to receive an abun-
dance of natural light.

Opposite Both private and common
areas throughout the home give a
sense of engagement with the outdoor spaces.

Spaces for Pleasure

NATALIA BAZAIOU STUDIO FOR ARCHITECTURE AND RESEARCH brings whimsy, discovery and greenery into the renovation of her 1970s family home called BARBARELLA HAS LIVED HERE

Cathy Cunliffe

The large, full-height terrarium at the heart of the main living area puts on display plants, trees and soil.

Above **Filtered light comes through the terrarium, plunging the common areas in a natural sense of life.**

Opposite **Playful details are dispersed throughout the flat, adding layers onto the textures of various materials belonging to both the old structure as well as the new remodelling.**

ATHENS — When renovating her 1970s flat in the Greek capital, architect Natalia Bazaiou was faced with a familiar dilemma: a dark, cellular layout and a limited budget. As with any flat, there are limited opportunities for contact with the natural world, let alone enough outdoor space for play.

Undeterred, Bazaiou has solved her first problem by creatively reusing her family's vintage furniture and scavenging materials and components from other projects. This sustainable approach results in an unexpected collage of elements and surfaces – a coffee table on chunky castors, bright yellow monkey bars running the length of a hallway, or even a miniature climbing wall in one of the rooms. Underfoot, there is a mixture of parquet floors, terracotta tiles, wood, smooth concrete and even pebbles. This playfulness is however underpinned by a more serious intent – to give the family a space that stimulates a sense of discovery.

Another significant intervention was to position a large, lush, full height terrarium in the home, creating a subtle division within the open-space living area. 'Plants, trees and soil are the basic elements of life in this apartment,' according to the architect. Cultivating playfulness as well as plants, Bazaiou's Barbarella has lived here provides a blueprint for city living that fosters health and harmony through fun and a connection with the natural world.

Below **Reworked vintage furniture provides supplemental character to the lively spaces.**

Right **The sculptural simplicity of certain elements of the flat recall characteristics of the Greek landscape.**

Opposite below **Bright yellow monkey bars line the length of the hallway ceiling.**

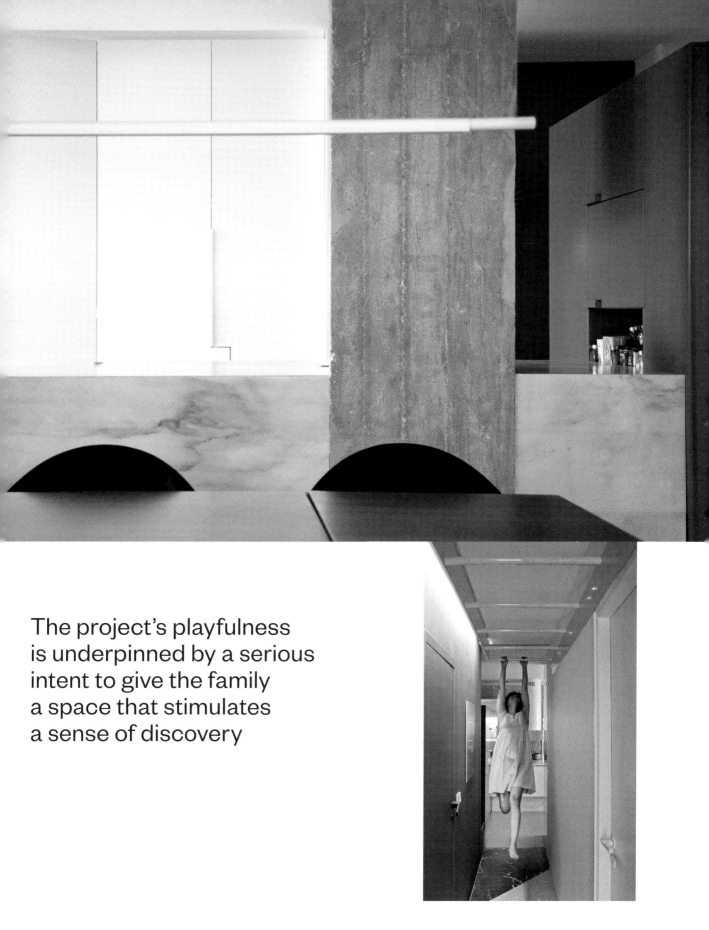

The project's playfulness is underpinned by a serious intent to give the family a space that stimulates a sense of discovery

The grey scheme of the building's concrete is contrasted with the surrounding gardens' greenery and warmth of the wooden interiors at the entrance of the complex.

RO_AR ARCHITECTS avoid nostalgia and 'exotic' clichés when adapting an old factory into YOGA GARDEN & ART GALLERY BRNO

Skylights flood the interior spaces with natural light.

BoysPlayNice

BRNO — In Yoga Garden & Art Gallery Brno, studio RO_AR architects combines two seemingly unrelated functions within an old factory in the middle of an urban block. Avoiding both the 'deceitful nostalgia' of some post-industrial spaces and 'false spirituality' of the typical European yoga studio, the architects rely on working with – and sometimes against – the found space.

In the first instance, the architects preserved the factory's skylights and timber beams that support the roof. Inside, white render is applied to most walls and ceilings, though a select few are left in their distressed, damaged state. The architects have also inserted two green patios within the structure, opening views of planting from the yoga studios and retaining rainwater run-off. New partition walls have been erected to divide the space into its functional components and a column has been eliminated in one of the studios, creating an uninterrupted area for exercise.

Sharing a generous entrance hall, the gallery is functionally separate from the exercise spaces, but sliding doors and slanting windows in the inner walls allow a more open connection towards the exterior. Underfoot, poured concrete floor in the gallery and studio foyer contrasts with the more comfortable parquet and cork floor in the two studios. The scheme's hybrid programme, but singular architectural approach, creates an environment that balances culture with exercise and old with new.

Following the demolition of a concrete pillar, the wooden binding beam 'levitates' in its incredible length as if defying gravity, which is further accentuated by the crossing LED light strip.

Original timbering was reinforced with steel and supplemented with new wooden structures, providing the entrance with a sense of warmth.

The gallery is functionally separate from
the exercise spaces, but sliding doors
allow an open connection towards a patio

Right **Fragments of the old building were demolished in order to
make space for gardens.**

Below **Large windows within
the yoga studio provide views of
the adjacent trees and gardens.**

Opposite **The wear and tear of
the building's original plastering,
conserved and partly cleaned,
gives authenticity to the space.**

Yoga Garden & Art Gallery Brno by RO_AR architects

STUDIO PUISTO's SAUNARAVINTOLA KIULU combines wellness and hospitality on a Finnish lakefront

Marc Goodwin

Above **The structure is nestled into the landscape, blending in with its environment.**

Opposite **The wellness centre's master plan actively engages with the lakefront.**

ÄHTÄRI — According to the architects at Studio Puisto, the concept for the new sauna and restaurant Saunaravintola Kiulu is a contemporary take on 'mummolan rantasauna'. This translates as your 'grandma's sauna on a lake' and is meant to evoke cosy, carefree comforts, while serving as a new social space for locals and visitors alike.

The project is no simple pastiche, however – the architects have created an expansive stepped terrace out of pale wood facing the lakefront. It extends into two asymmetrical jetties, while the restaurant space sits in the centre, its floor-to-ceiling windows revealing panoramic views of the water. A wide stair on one side leads to a roof terrace, while the sauna block on the other side is clad in dark timber planks. This

sophisticated simplicity can be found inside the restaurant too, where the warm tones of pale wood are complemented by a robust, red brick floor, natural cotton curtains and moulded plywood chairs.

Just like the outside, the inside of the sauna block is also clad in black wooden planks, creating a more intimate atmosphere. As another part of this complex, one small sauna stands more independently, creating an opportunity for smaller-scale gatherings. The floor is coated in epoxy, featuring the same hue as the brick in the restaurant, which creates a sense of continuity. With its own entrance and outdoor access, guests can make use of the facility at their own convenience, emphasising the project's casual, convivial aspect.

Saunaravintola Kiulu by Studio Puisto

Below **The sauna's floor is levelled with the outside to make the transition between outside and inside seamless.**

Opposite **The dark timber planks of the secluded saunas help foster a feeling of intimacy and relaxation.**

Riikka Kantinkoski

Spaces for Pleasure

Marc Goodwin

Warm tones of pale wood are complemented by a robust, red brick floor, natural cotton curtains and moulded plywood chairs

Riikka Kantinkoski

Marc Goodwin

Above Furniture along the steps, all the way to the building's roof, provide opportunities for lounging and dining while taking advantage of the scenic views.

Right Ceiling-height windows help spa-goers form a connection with the water while relaxing in the sauna.

Opposite Pale tones and floods of light within the spa's restaurant create a soft, warm ambiance, complemented by the traditional red brick used as tiling on the floor.

Saunaravintola Kiulu by Studio Puisto

Bookworms rejoice – WUTOPIA LAB's recipe for employee wellbeing at a Chinese online retailer HQ is the poetic SATORI HARBOR LIBRARY

GUANGZHOU — Employee wellbeing has been at the forefront of office design, but the trend has largely targeted physical wellbeing as a route to improved mental health – think ping-pong tables, slides, yoga rooms or even ball pits. Wutopia Lab's Satori Harbor Library at the Chinese online retailer VIP HQ bypasses the physical and goes straight for the cerebral.

Spread over two storeys, the design of the library is inspired by the Taoist principle of Satori/Zhaoche – an attainable, momentary state of enlightenment – as well as the history of Guangzhou as China's sole trading port with the West. Rounded, cave-like portals take the visitor from the lift lobby into the library, laid out along the centre of the building's core. The fully glazed perimeter is conceived as a communal reading space rendered in concrete and terrazzo and is inspired by the shores of the nearby Pearl River. A dock becomes a small amphitheatre, the curving riverbank a series of stepped benches. Wutopia Lab has even marooned an enormous longboat with a moving red sail divider within the library, providing seating and structure to the space.

A contemplative, organically formed grotto completes this sequence of spaces, offering employees a chance, even if momentarily, to focus their minds away from the earthly matters of work and enjoy a peaceful moment alone with their thoughts.

The architects forwent any distracting colours, textures and materials, unifying the 2000-m² library with desaturated beige stucco and terrazzo.

Right Manchuria windows dispersed throughout the library and floral-patterned tiles are fragments from the history of Guangzhou.

Below Many intimate corners along the corridor await to be appropriated by individual visitors.

Opposite Grotto-esque spaces allow for disorientation and deprivation of time and space.

The design of the library is inspired by the Taoist principle of Satori/Zhaoche – an attainable, momentary state of enlightenment

KEY TAKEAWAYS

1. Spaces for pleasure benefit from CLEAR NARRATIVES and concepts that help create spatial sequences and zones. These can be derived either from location or an interpretation of the brief.

2. Spaces for pleasure often BLUR THE BOUNDARIES BETWEEN THE OUTSIDE AND THE INSIDE, whether that's bringing greenery and physical activity into homes, or creating new social spaces that meld the two.

3. LESS CAN BE MORE. Designers should focus on creating a connection between the space, its inhabitants and the environment, rather than introduce ever more gadgets, gimmicks and digital connectivity.

4. The best green and healthy features are INTEGRAL TO A SPACE'S DESIGN, as well as MULTIFUNCTIONAL, providing additional spatial, visual and a raft of other benefits.

SPACES FOR

THE BODY

Below The relaxation room, featuring patches of soft pastel colours, curtain rails guided by precise tile grid and custom-made loungers, offers peaceful abstraction.

Opposite Large potted plants throughout the centre provide it with a living element and intimate atmosphere.

Sensory deprivation never felt so sensual as in BUREAU's pastel-coloured FLOATING REALITIES

Dylan Perrenoud

GENEVA — Sensory deprivation might not sound like a wellness concept at first, but a growing body of evidence suggests that an hour in a darkened flotation tank might help reduce anxiety levels and allow individuals to recalibrate and enhance their senses. In Floating Realities, Swiss-Portuguese office BUREAU takes visitors on a journey from the street to the pod, stripping away the everyday and taking the spa's clients on an 'intimate, timidly erotic and calm trip'.

The entrance is designed as a dreamy, street-side cafe, meticulously decked out in pastel tiles. Reclaimed park benches painted in matching colours and a dark rock emerging from the ceiling add a surrealist touch as visitors prepare to parse their unconscious mind.

Large indoor plants are scattered throughout the space to evoke an informal – almost unguarded – atmosphere.

From there, clients venture into a tiled relaxation room where they can strip down and recline on custom-made loungers divided by curtains. The curtain rails, shelves and lockers are guided by the precise tile grid and once again painted in matching, soft pastel colours. From this transition zone, they then enter individual womb-like floatation cells. With only soft ambient lighting, the journey is now complete. With its subtle dreamlike quality and masterful sequences of colour and space, Floating Realities facilitates a private journey into the self.

With its subtle dreamlike quality and masterful sequences of colour and space, Floating Realities facilitates a private journey into the self

Right **Various forms and pastel colours evoke a dreamy playfulness.**

Opposite **The centre's dream-like theme is maintained throughout its transition zones and practical elements, carefully guiding the client throughout the sensual journey.**

Below A mirror reflects the self-centred nature of the complex.

Right The intimate journey culminates in a salted water pod where users float, deprived of their physical senses, bathed in soft ambient lighting.

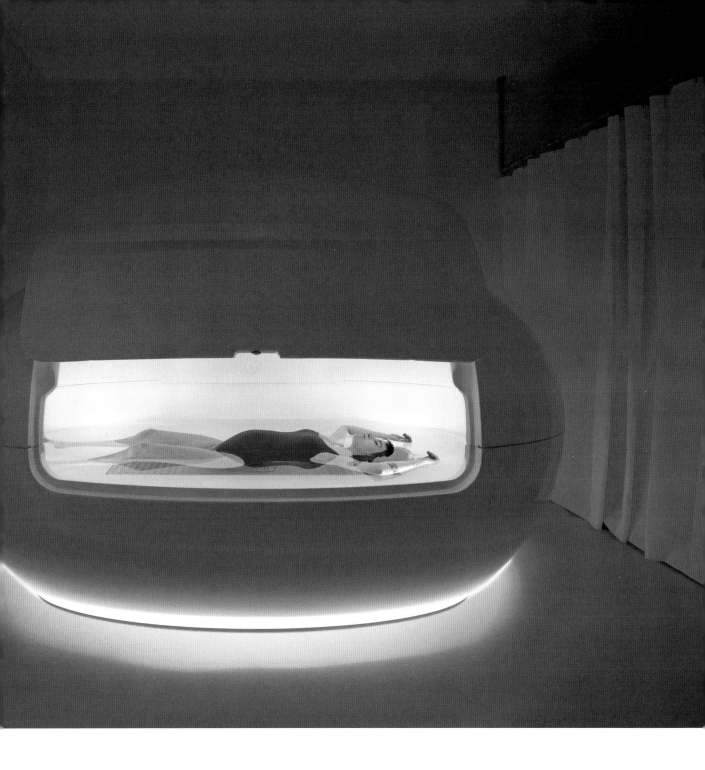

Visitors enter individual floatation cells – with only soft ambient lighting, the journey is now complete

The entrance is designed as a street-side cafe, featuring pastel tiles and refurbished 20th-century park benches.

Inspired by Singapore's cosmopolitan spirit, kfuna's toki + LIM hair salon is an inclusive space for self-care

The gently curving walls
transform the salon into
a self-contained maze.

The concrete structures create spaces ideal for fostering a one-on-one connection between staff and customers.

SINGAPORE — Visiting the hairdresser is and probably always has been as much about self-care as it is about people-watching. Inspired by Singapore's cosmopolitan spirit, where different cultures, religions and peoples mix with apparent ease, Japanese architecture studio kfuna has designed a new hair salon toki + LIM. The diversity of the Asian trading hub as well as the design's ethos is even reflected in the name – 'toki' contains the Chinese characters for sun and moon, symbolising balance and difference, while 'LIM' is an acronym of 'less is more'.

Both of these principles are carried through into the design. Located within the historic and iconic colonial-era Raffles Hotel, the salon comprises a small, self-contained maze of gently curving walls. Not all are full height and none quite give full enclosure – that's the point. Kfuna's design expresses the balance between privacy and coexistence. It allows staff to focus and customers to relax, while also creating moments of visual connection as people move through the space.

Rough concrete walls, timber shelves and cabinets as well as robust grey seats all create a tranquil setting for both customers and staff. The strength of the design lies in channelling peaceful coexistence and an egalitarian spirit – even if each space is slightly different – and reflecting this using a simple material and colour palette in addition to subtle spatial gestures.

The combination of concrete and timber gives the salon an air of tranquillity, while reflecting the salon's ethos.

Although the salon fosters an egalitarian spirit, each private space is slightly different.

The strength of
the design lies in
channelling peaceful
coexistence and
an egalitarian spirit

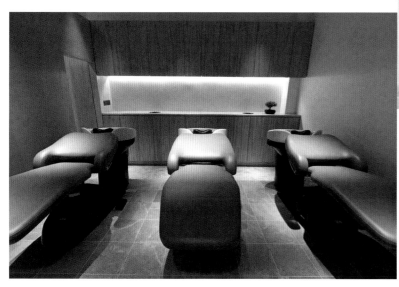

Above **The concrete walls act as partitions, balancing both privacy and coexistence.**

Opposite **Customers can fully relax while getting their hair washed and treated in the dimly lit space.**

toki + LIM by kfuna

The availability of open spaces allows for a versatile range of approaches to freelance hairdressing.

Ota Takumi

kfuna's JAM brings a raw, individualistic spirit to the world of freelance hairdressing

OSAKA — As the ranks of freelancers grow, so does the demand for shared workspaces. In Japan's third city, a new type of space, JAM, caters to freelance hairdressers. It allows them to set their own working hours or even split their time between private appointments off-site and a more permanent space for regular customers and walk-ins.

Designed by local architecture practice kfuna, the shared salon provides a number of spaces that can be rented by freelance hairdressers, as well as more basic workstations set out along a blank wall. The concept for the space is a 'jam', a place, according to the architects, where 'different people work alongside each other' and where there is very little hierarchy due to the ad-hoc nature of the work. This is reflected in the angled partition walls that separate the individual workspaces which are alternatively clad in wood wool board, MDF planks and ceramic tiles.

A dedicated photo space provides the customers and hairdressers with a neutral space to take photographs for social media if they wish to. The waiting area features iridescent glass and small round desks, just about big enough to balance a laptop on. The salon's clientele is just as connected and on the run as the hairdressers, meaning that the new space can fit seamlessly into their busy lifestyles.

The concept for the space is 'jam', a place where 'different people work alongside each other'

Left The glowing wall situated at the entrance varies in colour depending on the angle, reflecting the concept of individuality and difference in perspectives.

Below Pops of bright colour contrast with the concrete floors and ceilings.

Bottom The use of partitions allow versatility in the use of the salon's spaces.

Glass partitions double as a waiting area equipped with round table tops just big enough for clients to rest their laptop on.

Below Holed partition walls provide privacy for individual workspaces, while allowing professionals to determine the availability of the space.

Opposite A variety of materials is employed for the partition walls, again recalling the idea of individuality and eliminating a hierarchy of materials.

Angled partition walls separating the individual workspaces are clad in wood wool board, MDF planks and ceramic tiles

kfuna's design for a 'modest and elegant' beauty salon ONE & ONLY combines Japanese architectural tradition with bold contemporary forms

Opposite **Traditional elements, such as the 'genkan', were preserved throughout the house.**

Above **A wooden lattice provides the clients with privacy while recalling traditional 'machiya' screenwork.**

Above **The large circular window added onto the house's facade provides the salon with a light-filled interior space.**

Opposite **Warm pink walls differentiate the new from the old.**

OSAKA — Japanese vernacular architecture is admired all around the world. So, it comes as no surprise that when kfuna was asked to convert the ground floor of an old 'machiya' townhouse into a beauty salon, tradition would be a major source of inspiration for the design of the space.

Kfuna has simplified the ground floor layout and opened up the space, while retaining traditional elements, such as the 'genkan', a Japanese stepped entry hall, which doubles as a timber-clad waiting room complete with a built-in bench. The architects have also added a large circular window in the house's originally blank facade, creating a light-filled salon space in the front room. A lattice helps maintain clients'

privacy and makes a contemporary nod to traditional 'machiya' screenwork.

Beyond, the space curves toward the house's former main reception room. Here, with a full view of the small rock garden, customers have their hair washed and treated opposite the original 'tokonoma', the niche that contains 'ikebana' flower arrangements or hanging scrolls in a traditional Japanese home. The new walls are painted a warm pink to differentiate them from the older parts of the structure. Together with stainless steel accents, pale timber panelling and a tiled floor, they bring a contemporary spirit to this historical renovation.

Kfuna has simplified the ground floor layout and opened up the space, while retaining many traditional elements

A small rock garden is in full view of the customers, providing them with a sense of tranquility as they enjoy their day of self-care.

A new BICYCLE PARKING GARAGE IN THE HAGUE by creative agencies SILO and STUDIOMARSMAN takes cues from the surrounding cityscape

THE HAGUE — In the last two decades, major Dutch train stations and the areas around them have undergone significant updates in order to accommodate the growing number of passengers. Adjacent bicycle parking facilities have been greatly expanded too, providing a safe, convenient space for commuters to park their bikes, encouraging active and sustainable travel, while reducing car use in city centres. It's not just about the ease of access and functionality – eye-catching yet considered design has been instrumental in attracting new users by providing a safe and secure parking experience.

The new underground cycle parking garage connected to The Hague's Central Station provides space for 8000 bicycles, accessed using a series of convenient escalator ramps. The internal envelope features a large-scale mural designed by creative agency Silo, based on M.C. Escher's *Metamorphosis*. The black-and-white graphic takes inspiration from the city's landmarks and also serves as a subtle, ever-changing and intuitive wayfinding device. More conventional wayfinding signs, consistent with those in the train station above are suspended from the ceiling, creating an obstacle free ground plane, while LED counters point cyclists towards free spaces.

Together with white floors and ceilings, even levels of white lighting throughout and impactful visuals, the space feels spacious, secure, and compellingly alive. By creating an attractive cycle parking environment, the project aims to make commuters' experience as convenient and pleasant as possible.

A series of escalator ramps provides access to the underground parking garage.

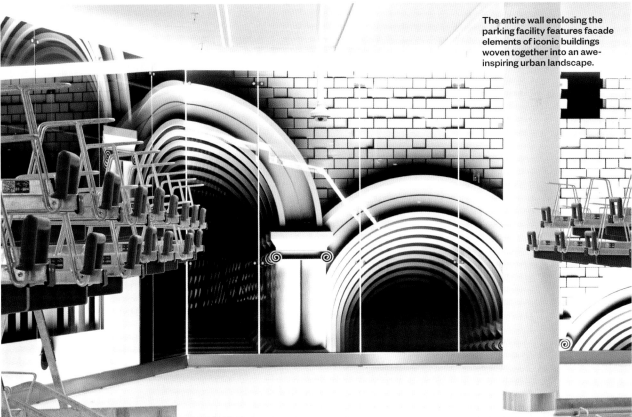

The entire wall enclosing the parking facility features facade elements of iconic buildings woven together into an awe-inspiring urban landscape.

Bicycle parking garage The Hague by Silo and studiomarsman

Above The integrated application of light brightens the garage while giving the illusion of spaciousness.

Below Warm lighting throughout the facility creates a welcome contrast to the normally dim underground parking spaces.

Opposite The extra high, bright white ceiling, smart directional markings, spacious aisles and back-lit glass walls direct cyclists while providing them with a unique and pleasant experience.

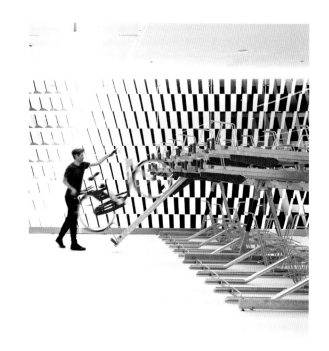

Eye-catching design has been instrumental in attracting new users by providing a safe and secure experience

Simple material gestures and colour palette allowed SIVAK+PARTNERS to design a striking centre point for THE KULT STUDIO

ODESSA — Combining a unisex barbershop with a tattoo parlour and a nail salon, The Kult Studio is the ultimate self-care space in Ukraine's famed seaside resort. The client's brief called for a unified and contemporary approach, eschewing the clichéd vintage look of many salons. In addition, the architecture studio Sivak+Partners was given only 3 months from starting the design to delivery.

Instead, the architects along with lead designer Ivanna Gaidarzhy have created a space that resembles a minimalist yet sophisticated boutique store. The main vaulted room has been designed in rough grey plaster, which creates a restrained atmosphere with matching angular barber chairs taking centre stage. The reception at the back of the space features a black polished marble desk, which adds luxury and creates a focal point, while a stainless-steel wall with custom-made shelves allows hair-care products to be displayed. Together, these three elements create an aesthetic of strong contrasts within a highly restricted palette.

A small waiting area located on top of the mezzanine, featuring low slung sofas, gives customers a view of the hair salon, but also keeps the main space free of obstructions. The other spaces – the tattoo studio and nail parlour – are in the smaller, more closed off rooms to the side. The black and grey colour palette unifies the project, but crucially, given time constraints, allowed the architects to concentrate on designing the central reception area, which forms the centrepiece of the whole project.

The barbershop's restricted palette and angularity allowed the project to be completed within a tight deadline.

Right Black-coloured details
create dimension while remaining
within the barbershop's theme.

Opposite The reflective stainless-steel wall displaying various
hair products adds light and contrast to the monochrome space.

Below Angularity is recalled in the
overhead lighting fixtures.

The main vaulted room has been rendered in rough grey plaster, which creates a restrained atmosphere

The large blue iron lattice structure allows clients to personalise their fitness routine.

Colourful and whimsical, STUDIO RAMOPRIMO's M-FIT SPACE 01 gives visitors the freedom to choose their routine

A large steel slide spirals around the basement staircase, adding fun and playfulness into the users' workouts.

Above **The vaulted red niche provides a space for one-on-one training.**

Opposite **A bright red changing room reflects the fitness centre's playfulness and energetic spirit.**

BEIJING — The Studio Ramoprimo-designed M-Fit Space 01 is a whimsical gym and fitness studio which fuses fun with functionality. The colourful interior invites exercisers to inhabit the innovative fitness landscape in wildly different and personal ways, providing the freedom to work out in any way they might wish.

On entry, visitors are greeted by a stainless-steel reception desk, which gives way to a workout space divided by a curving blue grid. This permeable barrier offers supports for hanging ropes and hooks, as well as screening gym-goers and structuring spaces throughout. Downstairs, the main space is flanked by a bright red changing room and a black-mosaic toilet.

Blue lattices line the walls, echoing the space upstairs and a vaulted, vermillion niche provides a quiet place for one-on-one fitness instruction.

The architect's playfulness is not just restricted to colour choices – users can reach the basement by a spiral staircase, a swirling stainless-steel slide dropping four metres down and even a climbing wall. Classes are held in a separate, brick-clad room, and colour-adjustable lighting allows users to create an atmosphere most suited to their mood. By allowing users freedom to establish their own routine and providing a sense of fun, Studio Ramoprimo hopes to lure them back to the gym time and time again.

Hydroponic planters within
the breakout spaces filter out
particulates in the air.

Spaces for the Body

STUDIO REAKTOR brings a green-thumbed approach to the streamlined machines that are the LIVESPORT OFFICES

Robust perforated metal screens offer privacy, without entirely closing off the meeting rooms.

PRAGUE — Livesport, also known as Flashscore outside of the Czech Republic, is a global sports results aggregator and publisher where speed and accuracy are of the essence. The brand's new office had to become 'a space accelerating thoughts, making work easier and connecting people like cogs in a machine,' according to the architects at Studio Reaktor. This resulted in a high-performance workspace where efficiency and wellbeing are completely in sync.

The office is laid out in three concentric zones that span between an all-glass facade and a large internal atrium. Open-plan workspaces and collaboration areas benefit from direct daylight, while the middle zone consists of meeting rooms, concentration pods and kitchenettes that act as dividers with the final 'leisure zone' of informal breakout spaces facing the atrium. Corners and fittings are streamlined to allow more direct routes through the office and meeting rooms feature robust perforated metal screens that mediate between privacy while offering glimpses of the activity inside.

Despite its precise, machine-like styling, Studio Reaktor's design pays attention to the employees' wellbeing. All individual workstations are designed with ergonomic principles and are fully adjustable, while the breakout spaces are divided using hydroponic planters filtering out particulates in the air. Planters near the kitchenettes feature edible, fragrant herbs like broadleaf thyme, mint or lemon balm, encouraging employees to take a moment and brew a cup of fresh tea.

Left Corners and fittings are streamlined to allow more direct routes through the office.

Below Ergonomic principles were employed throughout the design of all spaces.

Opposite Kitchenettes throughout the office break up the leisure zones.

Livesport's new office is 'a space accelerating thoughts, making work easier and connecting people like cogs in a machine'

Livesport Offices by Studio Reaktor

Naomichi Sode

Right The shape of the building gradually expands in both elevation and plan from the front to the back.

Opposite Occupants are given the impression that they are walking along a path between the buildings, like a passage.

Architecture studio TAKUYAHOSOKAI combines the need for privacy with abundant natural light in the FIGURE GROUND hair salon

NIIGATA — Located in a dense, residential suburb not far from the city centre, the Figure Ground hair salon by TAKUYAHOSOKAI is shaped both by the area's urban morphology and by the need to create an intimate, soothing space where customers can relax while having their hair cut and treated.

The salon stands on a narrow plot between two houses. Its form of progressively larger cuboid volumes reflects the fragmentation of the streetscape, characterised by protruding garages and porches as well as the irregular shapes of Japan's residential architecture. Internally, however, the spaces line up along a central corridor, the ceiling height increasing as the customer progresses deeper into the salon.

The programme is also articulated along this sequence, beginning with a waiting room, staff area, hair cutting room, shampoo and relaxation space, then culminating in a small gallery which is functionally divided from the rest of the building.

North-facing windows bring in soft, diffuse light and their precise placement – either on the side of the building, as clerestory windows or close to the ground – ensures privacy for both the hairdresser and their clients. A simple polished concrete floor and whitewashed walls highlight the fluid nature of the space, as do oblique views across the building through its several patios, which help foster a tranquil, relaxing atmosphere.

Right **The project is made of multiple volumes.**

Opposite **The use of each section of the building was determined by the amount of natural sunlight obtained, as waiting, cutting and washing do not all require the same light.**

A simple polished concrete floor and whitewashed walls highlight the fluid nature of the space

Adjoining a cosmetic surgery, TEAM55667788's ATOP BEAUTY CLINIC lets visitors define what good looks mean to them

SEOUL — Even though South Koreans undergo the most plastic surgery per capita of any country in the world, the industry is increasingly keen to project a more holistic and wholesome image centred on wellbeing as well as self-fulfilment. ATOP Beauty Clinic – part of a larger cosmetic health centre – is a consultation space where patients and doctors can discuss various surgical and non-surgical procedures in a friendly, relaxing environment.

Colour plays a major role in the design conceived by TEAM55667788 – a textured coat of pastel peach-coloured paint covers the walls as well as the ceiling, while the floor features a material in the same hue, only more reflective. Even lighting uses the same colour, reinforcing the warm, monochrome effect.

A number of 'care zone' pods, screened off using grey felt partitions, offer semi-private spaces for consultation and treatment without compromising the feeling of openness. Containing a bed for the patients and a side seat for a consultant, the small, sheltered module creates an intimate zone designed to build trust between the client and the professional. Fully private consultation rooms are to the side and visitors can re-apply their make-up in a designated booth after their visit. A low shelf running around the perimeter of the space features a changing, carefully curated selection of decorative objects, inviting clients to contemplate the singular nature of beauty.

The waiting area offers clients a preview of the relaxing pods in which they will soon receive their treatments.

Colour plays a major role in the design and even the lighting reinforces the warm, monochrome effect

Below **Grey felt partitions offer semi-private spaces for consultation and treatment without compromising the feeling of openness.**

Opposite **The painting of rough texture similar to earthenware has been added to the arched ceiling and walls.**

ATOP Beauty Clinic by TEAM55667788

Right The small, sheltered module creates an intimate zone designed to build trust between the client and the professional.

Below Various materials are employed throughout the clinic, bringing texture to the space.

Opposite Backlit stone stylobates provide ambient lighting, bringing tranquillity and warmth.

The bright red reception
desk contrasts the grey
scheme of the concrete
walls and columns.

Oculis Project

Combining a fight-club aesthetic with a nightclub glamour, VSHD DESIGN's WAREHOUSE GYM SPRINGS is a stylish space to shape up

Coffered ceilings overhead
the workout spaces provide a
grid for lighting installations.

Spaces for the Body

Large backlit circular mirrors optically extend the space to infinity and beyond.

DUBAI — With ever more varied offerings, high-end gyms provide more than just some training equipment and a place to change and shower – especially in Dubai, where no amount of glitz and glamour can ever be too much. Conceived by VSHD Design, Warehouse Gym Springs is a combination of an underground fight club and a nightclub – the gym often hosts live DJs during the workout sessions – wrapped in a robust, brutalist-inspired formal language.

Located in a shopping centre, the space relies on the skilful integration of lighting and interior architecture. Concrete columns and beams are exposed and used to define the various workout zones within the space, with a coffered ceiling overhead concealing the gym's adaptable lighting installation. Meanwhile, large backlit circular mirrors optically extend the space to infinity and beyond. Retro-futurism gives way to fully retro in the tiled changing rooms – with oxblood and white tiles, brass pendant lights, powder-blue shelves and cabinets as well as timber shower doors.

In this gym, substance and style blend seamlessly – providing a space for serious exercise, while allowing visitors to post those all-important pre-, during and post-workout selfies. After all, if you go to the gym without posting it on social media, did you really go to the gym at all?

If you go to the gym without posting it on social media, did you really go to the gym at all?

Above and right The oxblood and white tiles give the changing rooms a retro feel.

Opposite The retro tiles are complemented by brass pendant lights and powder-blue details.

Customers in YASUHIRO SAWA DESIGN OFFICE's MARE EYEDESIGN beauty salon enjoy views of the adjacent park's cherry blossom

KYOTO — Such is the cherry blossom's importance in Japanese culture, that yasuhiro sawa design office's concept for MARE eyedesign, a small brow and lash salon in central Kyoto, is wholly focused on framing the views of the adjacent park, offering customers a relaxing panorama of white petals for a few weeks each year.

As the salon is located on the first floor of a larger building, the principal facade consists of large windows which flood the space with light and allow views of the outside without passers-by looking in. By incorporating the park into the design of the space, it almost acts as a piece of 'borrowed scenery', a technique often used in East Asian landscape and architectural design, bringing the outside in.

The reception area consists of a terrazzo counter and a curving mustard yellow wall. This organic curve continues as a curtain rail, helping subdivide the space and ensuring privacy for clients and employees. The sheer curtain preserves the interior's airy, ethereal atmosphere, while simple, timber partitions, suspended from the ceiling, separate the individual treatment spaces and a concrete floor throughout completes the minimally designed space. At the same time, the flexible curtain allows for several possibilities depending on the employee's and customer's mood, revealing a hint of playfulness and whimsy.

The adjacent park offers the salon's clients views of cherry blossoms for the period of a few weeks every year.

MARE
eyedesign

Akari Kuramoto

Above The curve of the reception's wall continues organically as the curtain railing.

Right The terrazzo counter complements the minimal concrete floor and exposed beams.

The incorporation of the park into the design of the space means it acts as a piece of 'borrowed scenery', a technique often used in East Asian landscape and architectural design

MARE eyedesign by yasuhiro sawa design office

This small brow and lash salon in central Kyoto is wholly focused on framing the views of the adjacent park

Below and left The sheer curtains allow for privacy within the treatment spaces, while preserving the salon's airy, ethereal atmosphere.

Bottom The large windows overlooking the park incorporate its views into the salon, acting as a piece of 'borrowed scenery'.

MARE eyedesign by yasuhiro sawa design office

KEY TAKEAWAYS

1. Many of these spaces lack natural light by design, meaning the most successful projects use this opportunity to CREATE SURREAL INTERIOR DREAM WORLDS, allowing clients to escape from their everyday realities.

2. MULTIFUNCTIONAL AND INTERACTIVE ELEMENTS WITHIN DESIGNS, from ramps to storage racks can double as space dividers or displays and help to save room while creating a strong identity and affinity with users.

3. While INSTAGRAM MOMENTS should not be a guiding principle for spatial design, their inclusion within the overall scheme can enhance user experience and satisfaction and can help owners with word-of-mouth advertising and marketing.

4. CLEAR CIRCULATION AND ZONING will help optimise the use of the space, both for individuals as well as groups of users.

SPACES FOR

CONNECTING

A transparent, ground-floor yoga studio at ADEMÁS ARQUITECTURA's MARÍA RAFAELA HOSTEL creates a peaceful retreat for travellers

BUENOS AIRES — Mindfulness retreats are often the stuff of luxury holidays, but there is no reason why more modest accommodation can't also offer its guests a generous amount of space dedicated to inner balance. In the Argentine capital, Además Arquitectura has realised the María Rafaela Hostel, a respite for weary travellers with a yoga studio and a communal roof terrace.

Located within a large, mature garden belonging to an existing villa, the architects have situated the yoga studio on the ground floor, with direct access to the yard. Expansive, curved floor-to-ceiling glazing creates a direct visual connection to the outside, while large ceramic floor tiles give the impression of a communal, indoor plaza with an open dialogue with the exterior.

On the side, a volume containing the reception, store rooms and a staircase is clad in grey and rust-coloured ceramic tiles. Upstairs, the hostel's five rooms feature angled bay windows to ensure maximum insolation. This chamfered volume clad in orange brown brick contrasts and seems to float above the ethereal, glazed pavilion below. The top of the building accommodates a communal roof terrace, giving visitors a more expansive view of the surrounding leafy suburbs. By introducing a wellness function within a relatively humble hospitality venue, the architects demonstrate the broad possibilities when it comes to creating hybrid spaces.

Gonzalo Viramonte.

Grey and rust-coloured
ceramic tiles clad the exterior
of the volume containing the
reception area, store rooms
and staircase.

María Rafaela Hostel by Además Arquitectura

227

Large ceramic floor tiles create an impression of a communal, indoor plaza with an open dialogue with the world outside

Above The expansive, curved floor-to-ceiling glazing of the yoga studio creates a direct visual connection to the outside.

Right The plaza's curved windows give a sense of transparency and playfulness.

Opposite Dense vegetation and brick walls hold the old villa, composed now of five rooms all facing north.

Above The scattering of the
modules throughout the forest
allows for forest preservation
and full immersion into nature.

Opposite The modules are raised
on stilts, eliminating the need
for a concrete foundation.

BoysPlayNice

ARK-SHELTER's modular cabins for SHELTERS FOR HOTEL BJORNSON combine formal simplicity with sustainable materials

DEMÄNOVSKÁ DOLINA — This small holiday resort in central Slovakia, consisting of a series of cabins designed by Ark-Shelter for Hotel Bjornson, is highly attuned to the natural world. It intends to provide visitors to the nearby ski resort with a simple, back-to-basics experience.

The prefabricated timber cabins are built on stilts, allowing the landscape and undergrowth to flow freely underneath. Pine trees cluster around the site and between some of the cabins. The interiors are simple, containing the main living space with a sofa and a double bed, separated by a curtain, a bathroom and an alcove for children. Pale timber dominates the living and sleeping spaces, with only the grey sofa and armchair upholstery as well as slender black light fixtures providing contrast.

As the cabins are arranged in pairs, two adjoining modules can be combined to form a larger, multifamily suite using sliding doors, or they can function wholly independently. A skylight in the middle of the plan brings in additional natural light. Some larger cabins offer a balcony, and all guests can use a communal sauna featuring a large floor-to-ceiling window with a view of the forest. Taken together, the pared-back accommodation is not just about unspoilt nature – after all, the cabins are right next to the ski slope – but rather about being immersed in the moment without any unnecessary distractions.

Turning an old hospital into KIRO HIROSHIMA BY THE SHARE HOTELS, HIROYUKI TANAKA ARCHITECTS retains the building's people-centred mission

HIROSHIMA — Converting an old hospital in the city centre into a hotel required 'an archaeological approach,' according to Hiroyuki Tanaka Architects. Instead of trying to squeeze as many 'extravagant' facilities as possible onto the constrained site, the architects have kept the building's simple, functional ethos and created a place where in-person interaction between visitors and locals becomes the design's primary focus. The hotel's name, KIRO, means 'crossroads' in Japanese, alluding to the hotel's objective of being a meeting place for travellers on their journeys.

Traces of the building's past remain visible, be it in the generous dimensions of circulation spaces and doorways, large windows or the tiled surfaces that remain conserved throughout. The hotel's 49 rooms have been left consciously compact. Minimalist furnishings encourage guests to venture out and use the third-floor bar and lounge, situated in the hospital's centrally located rehabilitation pool.

Here, the tiled poolsides have been retained and patched up where necessary, but the space maintains the bright and airy feel of a conservatory, enhanced by the large indoor plants arranged along the perimeter. The pool has also been refloored and now functions as a conversation pit, becoming the focal point of the renewed building's social life.

The generous dimensions of the circulation spaces are remains from the building's past life as a hospital.

Gottingham

Below Japanese-style rooms are offered as an option for guests wishing to experience the 'real' Hiroshima.

Bottom The hotel maintains elements of the original building, such as the tiled walls in the lounge area.

Right The hotel's third-floor bar and lounge was reborn from the skeleton of what was previously a rehabilitation pool.

Traces of the building's past remain visible in generous circulation spaces and doorways, large windows and tiled surfaces

KIRO Hiroshima by THE SHARE HOTELS by Hiroyuki Tanaka Architects

The complex was designed to mimic a small village comprising easily recognisable buildings, all slightly different, yet cohesive.

Recognisable forms, traditional materials and familiar places are the key ingredients in NORDIC – OFFICE OF ARCHITECTURE's CARPE DIEM DEMENTIA VILLAGE

BÆRUM — In the United Kingdom, one in six people over the age of 80 have some form of dementia, which provides designers with a new set of challenges. While patients' needs are often complex and individual, many dementia sufferers can enjoy a relatively high standard of living if their housing allows it.

Just west of Oslo, Nordic – Office of Architecture has designed Carpe Diem Dementia Village, a new care home and assisted living facility tailored to those living with Alzheimer's and related conditions. Comprising 136 communal units and 22 high-care homes, the architects have created a finely grained microcosm of a small town. Individual, gabled houses stand around an internal, car-free courtyard, which is modulated to create streets, squares and gardens.

The two- and three-storey buildings are clad in different shades of brick or timber planks, while retractable awnings keep out the glare.

The dementia village provides a varied, yet recognisable and safe townscape with communal facilities, such as a hair salon, a supermarket, a cafe and a pub, in which residents can socialise and lead a more independent life. The outdoor areas can be used for exercise; the landscaping and various building forms and facades help navigating the village intuitively. Inside, a simple layout and colourful everyday furnishings create a pleasant environment that residents can identify with and which stands in stark contrast with the anonymous, institutional environments that are all too often used for elderly care.

Greenery-lined paved walkways throughout the village encourage physical activity within the safety of the complex.

Carpe Diem Dementia Village by Nordic – Office of Architecture

Below **Colourful everyday furnish-ings brighten the residents' lives.**

Opposite **A comforting feeling is achieved in communal spaces by integrating familiar materials into the design, such as wood, as well as earth-toned colours and inclusive design concepts.**

Inger Marie Grinil

Inside, a simple layout and colourful everyday furnishings create a pleasant environment that residents can identify with

Encouraging physical over digital connection, ODAMI's design for the pared-back restaurant SARA banishes mobile phones

TORONTO — While technology can foster instantaneous connections with the wider world, some behavioural scientists are increasingly worried that too much screen time can have a detrimental effect on the time we spend with our dearest and nearest. Prioritising physical connection in a calm environment, Canadian studio Odami designed Sara, a restaurant which is 'meant to be felt, not seen.'

The designers aimed to eliminate any visual noise in their design, be it graphic branding, or elaborate furnishing that would intrude on the space. Located in a Victorian townhouse, the restaurant comprises a more intimate, vaulted, roughly plastered ground floor, while the first floor makes use of the former attic space to create an airy, double-height space.

With simple wooden chairs and seafoam green upholstered banquette seating along the walls, the interior is uncluttered and simple, putting the focus on the food and the people within. The calm, pared-back interior may provide a suitable milieu to disconnect, but Odami has also created custom design for the dining tables that features a hidden compartment, encouraging diners to put away their mobile phones as part of a small ritual before the meal. Although the designers insist the space 'is all about the atmosphere', it is this attention to detail that allows them to create a genuine space for real human interactions, allowing customers to switch off.

Kurtis Chen

Dining tables
feature a hidden
compartment,
encouraging diners
to put away their
mobiles as part of
a pre-meal ritual

Various recycled materials are embedded in the plastered walls, creating a unique and intricate fossil-like design.

Sara by Odami

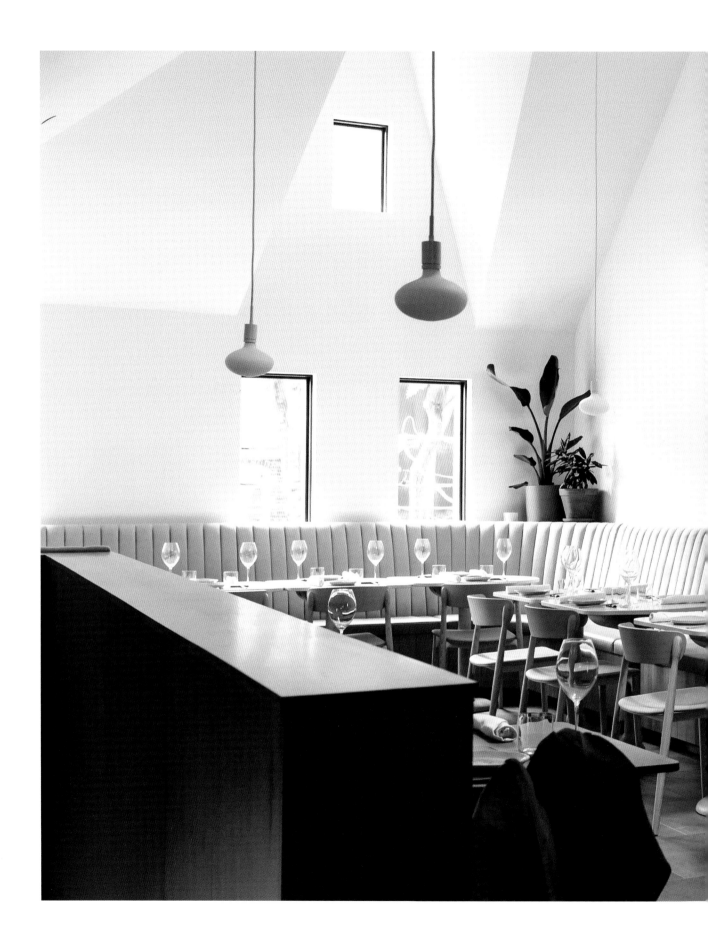

The first floor features pitched, double-height ceilings and clean white walls, fostering a light and airy atmosphere.

Bright colours and playful communal spaces define PROJECTS OFFICE's CHILD AND ADOLESCENT MENTAL HEALTH SERVICES facility in Edinburgh's Royal Hospital for Children and Young People

A central, orange-striped 'light-house' creates a focal point, while the false skylight above adds light and height to the space.

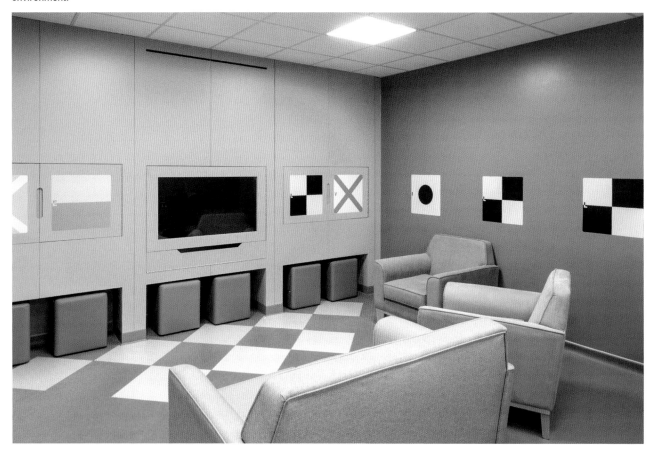

EDINBURGH — Designing within public health-care systems can be challenging at the best of times. With tightly prescriptive briefs and even tighter budgets, good design often isn't the highest priority. Thankfully, these attitudes are shifting, especially when a growing body of evidence highlights the positive impact of colour, views and communal facilities on patient experience and wellbeing.

Nowhere is this more obvious than when designing spaces for mental health patients. In Edinburgh's new Royal Infirmary, London-based practice Projects Office designed a colourful, communal ward for the Child and Adolescent Mental Health Services (CAMHS). The project combines bright accent colours, such as orange and yellow, as well as cooler hues including teal and forest green to create an uplifting, playful environment. A false skylight in the middle of the inpatients' communal day space adds light and height to the space, while a centrally situated orange-striped 'lighthouse' creates a focal point, offering patients a place to withdraw while still maintaining visual contact with carers.

The scheme also features a number of colourful patient rooms, which are finished with open plywood shelving that allow for a degree of personalisation. Materials like linoleum and standard hospital furnishings have been reimagined with bright patterns and colours, proving that bespoke, uplifting design can be realised even within the strict parameters and budgets set by the National Health Service.

Colourful patient rooms featuring open plywood shelving allow for personalisation.

Left **A lighthouse mural recalls the space's marine inspiration.**

Below **The dining area maintains fun, seaside colours while floor-to-ceiling wooden partitions create privacy between diners.**

Opposite **Colourful arches house seating for the patients and carers.**

Materials like linoleum and standard hospital furnishings have been reimagined with bright patterns and colours

SIXSEVEN STUDIO combines Japanese minimalism with traditional Thai material in Bangkok's YUNOMORI ONSEN AND SPA

BANGKOK — Yunomori Onsen and Spa, designed by Sixseven Studio, combines the distinct wellness cultures of Japanese bathhouses and Thai massages. Centrally located on a narrow plot in the bustling Thai capital, the architects nevertheless managed to introduce a sense of calm into the project by turning inwards, while still bringing natural light into the interior.

The complex comprises an existing residential building on one end of the plot that has been retrofitted to contain various Thai massage areas and wellness rooms, as well as a new block accommodating the Japanese baths, pools and steam rooms on the other. Between them, a bamboo-filled courtyard serves as a quiet place for relaxation and contemplation, a place of connection between the two cultures.

While the internal layout is inspired by the fluid spatiality of Japanese interiors and includes a double-height lobby, a Japanese restaurant as well as smaller internal gardens with light-wells above, contemporary Thai architecture is reflected by the material palette of red brick, pale stone, textured concrete and warm wood. Bamboo is a recurring theme throughout, used as planting, as cladding material, as screens and even as formwork for concrete. Recessed lighting, accentuated by a few strategically placed lanterns, respects the integrity of the space, while judiciously framed views of indoor plants onto the green courtyard blur the boundaries between inside and out.

Bamboo-clad facades and indirect lighting plunges the treatment areas in a stress-free atmosphere.

Left The design on the superior floors reflects simplicity and uniformity with the use of natural slate stone, while the wooden details bring warmth to the space.

Opposite The lush courtyard garden serves as a peaceful common space between both buildings, also providing views of greenery for the facility's restaurant.

Below Bamboo is used as formwork for concrete, creating a unique, yet familiar texture.

Bamboo is a recurring theme throughout, used as planting, as cladding material, as screens and even as formwork for concrete

WATERFROM DESIGN
showcases traditional
herbal remedies in
Beijing's radically calm
EXHIBITION OF
FROZEN TIME

The glacial colour palette used by the architect gives the traditional Chinese remedies a cool, minimalist twist.

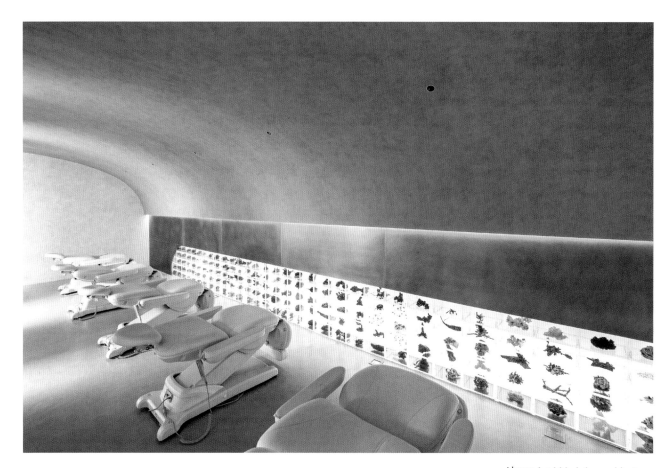

Above **A gridded glass cabinet containing almost 100 specimens of dried plants lines the wall of the treatment room.**

Opposite **The waiting room features a glazed terrarium bench.**

BEIJING — Despite its enduring popularity, traditional Chinese medicine evokes images of 'old cabinets and the smell of aged herbs,' according to Waterfrom Design. The studio's design for a Beijing spa and clinic, Exhibition of Frozen Time, intentionally subverts this image and gives traditional remedies a cool, minimalist twist.

The sparse entrance and waiting room, with its frosted glass reception booth and a glazed terrarium bench, sets the tone for the rest of the space. From there, visitors enter a boldly vaulted space that leads to the first treatment area devoted to facial care. Here, a row of medical recliners faces a gridded glass cabinet featuring almost 100 dried plant specimens used in traditional Chinese medicine as well as in the spa's treatments and cosmetics. Inspired by the art of Damian Hirst, these displays illustrate the timeless quality of these ancient remedies.

Visitors can opt for hair treatment in a glazed box, or retreat to more private areas beyond. Once their treatment is complete, they are guided to a small tearoom where they can relax and continue to enjoy the reviving properties of the various medicinal plants. The architects' use of a glacial colour palette throughout – green timber floors, grey and turquoise walls and vaults, complemented by occasional brass and ochre accents – creates a space for serious self-care amid Beijing's hustle and bustle.

KEY TAKEAWAYS

1. UNDERSTANDING AND ANTICIPATING the clients' and users' needs and wishes and the type of INTERPERSONAL CONNECTION they are aiming for can help in creating appropriately functional, but also decorative and artistic solutions to a project.

2. Refurbishing existing spaces, drawing on familiar spatial typologies as well as using local materials and iconography can create spaces with a STRONG LOCAL IDENTITY and SENSE OF CONNECTION.

3. It is paramount that any design fosters A SENSE OF COMMUNITY AND UTILITY – not only between the scheme's immediate users, but also implicitly serving the wider network of the city, town or village.

4. Designers need to focus on creating A FEELING OF SAFETY AND INCLUSIVITY in the broadest sense. The most successful projects create truly popular and accessible platforms for communal life, whether for specific activities, relaxation or other functions.

DESIGNER INDEX

100A ASSOCIATES
Seoul, South Korea
100a-associates.com

The philosophy of 100A associates is rooted in the studio's Korean heritage. The name 100A combines the meanings of ancient characters referring to the number 100 and the colour white respectively. 100A stands for a holistic approach, which considers the full scope of materiality, the potential held by empty space, as well as the conceptual essence of architecture.
page 8

2001
Esch-sur-Alzette,
Luxembourg
2001.lu

2001 is an architecture company. The abstraction of its name symbolises its ambitions to operate discreetly yet determinedly and serve strategically in the environment practiced by society. This environment defines its fields of interests, activities and scales: territories, buildings, spaces and ideas. 2001 was founded in 2010 by Philippe Nathan and is since 2014 led in partnership with Sergio Carvalho.
page 14

ADEMÁS ARQUITECTURA
Buenos Aires, Argentina
ademasarquitectura.com

Founded in 2007 by a group of students at the Faculty of Architecture, Design and Urban Design at the University of Buenos Aires, Además Arquitectura was and is about collective work. Led by Leandro Gallo and Florencia Speroni, the studio offers an opportunity for architects and students to work alongside each other. Devoted to constant learning and the search for theoretical and practical solutions, the practice engages in typological research and reformulating standard briefs. These concerns are complemented by a diligent investigation of material proposals in the resolution of architectural projects.
page 226

ALAN PREKOP
Bratislava, Slovakia
alanprekop.com

Alan Prekop founded his eponymous studio in Bratislava in 2020 after working with well-known Slovak architects, including Martin Skoček and studio GUTGUT. Prekop's work mainly focuses on housing, interiors, revitalisation and reconstruction of industrial buildings and interventions in public space as well as temporary and permanent installations. In addition to being an architect, Prekop is also a professional musician, leading to several high-profile collaborations with a number of Slovak music festivals designing events and pavilions.
page 86

ARHITEKT MUST
Tallinn, Estonia
arhitektmust.ee

Arhitekt Must is a group of young and creative architects. The studio, which currently brings together nine architects, was founded in 2013 by Ott Alver, Mari Rass and Alvin Järving. The main works in the studio have been achieved through the wins of public architectural competitions. At the moment the studio has completed two buildings and four are currently under construction. The first completed building – Suure-Jaani Health Center – has been nominated for the Mies Van der Rohe Award. The partners also supervise students in the architecture department of the Estonian Academy of Arts.
page 24

ARK-SHELTER
Lichtervelde, Belgium
ark-shelter.com

Ark-Shelter's mission is to reinvent the way people live their lives by connecting people to their biological roots. By incorporating nature within homes and workspaces, the architects aim to alleviate the stress of modern life. The practice's signature 'Arks' provide a low-tech shelter conceived as a cocoon and a place to reconnect with and appreciate nature. Made using sustainable materials and adaptable to their user's changing needs, the practice's projects aim to become an extension of the landscape.
page 230

A+R ARCHITEKTEN
Stuttgart, Germany
ackermann-raff.de

a+r Architekten stands for solid, environmentally compatible and future-oriented architecture with impressive expertise in the field of sustainable building – also in existing building contexts. Founded in 1985 by Gerd Ackermann and Hellmut Raff, the office with branches in Stuttgart and Tübingen mainly works for public-sector clients, industry and commerce, municipal housing companies and social institutions. The office focuses on using locally appropriate, ecological, functional and innovative construction methods.
page 18

ATELIER CARACAS
Caracas, Venezuela
ateliercaracas.com

Founded in 2015 by Julio Kowalenko and Rodrigo Armas, Atelier Caracas is a precociously productive studio based in Caracas, Venezuela. Operating as a platform for formal, aesthetic and cultural investigation spanning architecture, furniture and fashion, Atelier Caracas draws strong influences from pop culture and everyday found objects to create alluring spaces and installations, at once humorous, thought-provoking and symbolically charged.
page 94

AT-LARS
Jakarta, Indonesia
at-lars.id

Founded by Stephanie Larassati in 2016, AT-LARS (Atelier Larassati) is a progressive and contemporary practice that focuses on design and architecture – from buildings, public spaces and exhibitions. For Larassati, architecture is not about form or style but rather about its emotional connection with the users and environment; and its adaptability to the local contexts, social life and users. The studio creates spaces as a platform for sensorial and visceral experiences, developing unique ideas and creating memorable moments and formulating design strategies for every design task based on research, functionality and opportunity.
page 76

BUREAU
Geneva, Switzerland and Lisbon, Portugal
bureau.ac

BUREAU is a critical platform for spatial practice founded by Daniel Zamarbide, Carine Pimenta and Galliane Zamarbide. The studio's generic name accommodates a variety of research activities. The members react to and participate in shaping the surrounding physical, cultural and social environment with a critical standpoint and with an immersive attitude. BUREAU's work also includes furniture, editorial projects and design.
page 152

CARLOS ZWICK ARCHITEKTEN BDA
Berlin, Germany
carlos-zwick.de

Carlos Zwick Architekten BDA is a Berlin architecture firm that was founded in 1989. An international team of architects, engineers and designers works under the direction of Carlos Zwick, who has successfully implemented numerous projects for more than 30 years. Zwick studied architecture after completing his apprenticeship as a carpenter at the University of Applied Sciences in Munich. The team specialises mainly in residential projects – whether renovations or new builds – from conception through to design development and construction.
page 98

COOKFOX ARCHITECTS
New York, USA
cookfox.com

COOKFOX Architects was founded in 2003 by Rick Cook and Bob Fox to pursue beautiful, innovative and sustainable design. Now led by Rick and six partners, the firm's core mission is to create environmentally responsible, holistic and biophilic architecture that fosters occupant wellbeing and a healthy urban landscape. The studio's work ranges in scope from small jewel projects to complex urban transformations, spanning multifamily residential and single-family homes to institutional and commercial projects.
page 106

GG-LOOP
Amsterdam, the Netherlands
gg-loop.com

GG-loop is an Amsterdam-based multidisciplinary architecture practice established in 2014 by Giacomo Garziano. GG-loop draws on an international network, deriving its strength from a focus on biophilic design and putting users first when responding to the design brief. Projects range from product design to large-scale urban planning and design for the real estate, retail, infrastructure and culture industries. The studio's work is informed by biomimicry, natural processes, mathematical systems and musical proportions and conceived to be transformed over time, according to the evolving needs of the user.
page 112

HIROYUKI TANAKA
ARCHITECTS
Tokyo, Japan
hiroyukitanaka.com

Born in 1976, Hiroyuki Tanaka gained his Environment Design Master's degree from Keio University in 2003. Afterwards, he started working at Carbondale in Paris. He worked on the Louis Vuitton Malletier Store on the Avenue des Champs-Élysées as well as numerous other projects globally between 2003 and 2005. After returning to Japan, he established Hiroyuki Tanaka Architects in 2006.
page 234

INTEGRATED FIELD
Bangkok, Thailand
integratedfield.com

Integrated Field is a Thailand-based design office dedicated to finding the reason behind each project in order to understand its essence, guide the design process and ultimately develop a fitting design. IF was founded in 2011 by a group of friends consisting of architects, an interior architect, a landscape architect and an industrial designer, working together and integrating individual sector-specific knowledge into the studio's diverse projects.
page 30

KAUNITZ YEUNG
ARCHITECTURE
Sydney, Australia
kaunitzyeung.com

Kaunitz Yeung Architecture is an award-winning internationally recognised practice founded by David Kaunitz and Ka Wai Yeung. It combines their extensive commercial experience with David's knowledge of living in and working with communities. The result is architecture that places people at its centre and where good architecture does not need to necessarily be a luxury item. Their projects are bespoke solutions that sensitively respond to clients, stakeholders, end user requirements, site context and the budget.
page 36

kfuna
Osaka, Japan
kfuna.ltd

kfuna was established by Fumitaka and Naomi Kawanishi in March 2014. With Fumitaka as the sole designer, the studio has worked both domestically as well as internationally. The practice is dedicated to designing residential architecture and commercial interiors, as well as managing the construction from concept to the finished product. The studio undertakes a wide range of projects such as restaurants, clothing stores, as well as newly built detached houses and beauty salons.
page 160, 168, 176

LACROIX CHESSEX
Geneva, Switzerland
lacroixchessex.ch

Lacroix Chessex is a Swiss practice dedicated to architecture in the broadest sense. Founded in 2005 by Hiéronyme Lacroix and Simon Chessex and headquartered in Geneva, Switzerland, the office employs a team of 25 architects. The firm's most prominent completed projects include the Maison des Etudiants for the Graduate Institute in Geneva, the roof extension with 50 dwellings at the rue de Lausanne in Geneva and the Apartment buildings and crèche at the Caserne de Reuilly in Paris.
page 42

MONTALBA ARCHITECTS
Santa Monica, USA /
Lausanne, Switzerland
montalbaarchitects.com

Founded in 2004 by David Montalba, Montalba Architects is an award-winning, multidisciplinary practice based in Santa Monica, California and Lausanne, Switzerland. The studio's holistic and international approach combines client needs, site requirements, cultural and economic landscape to create environments that are both socially responsive and aesthetically progressive.
page 122

NATALIA BAZAIOU STUDIO
FOR ARCHITECTURE AND
RESEARCH
Athens, Greece
nataliabazaiou.com

Natalia Bazaiou Studio for Architecture and Research is a studio operating within the fields of architecture, interior design, participatory design and research. Bazaiou is enthusiastic about the kind of architecture that places human interaction at its centre, as well as about the symbiosis of architecture and nature. Every project is an opportunity to generate new ways of using and experiencing space, rooted in a deep understanding of the user's own vision and needs. The studio's projects are playful in nature, taking inquisitive paths to rethink norms.
page 126

NATASHA THORPE DESIGN
Montreal, Canada
natashathorpedesign.com

Natasha Thorpe is a multidisciplinary designer specialising in total design environments and object design. Dedicated to designing every aspect in and of an environment, her approach allows for a unique sensory experience that operates seamlessly and cohesively. The practice seeks to translate collective meaning and symbolism into impactful design that is context and setting-driven for every day and days of exception, for moments, whole lives and everything in between.
page 48

NORDIC – OFFICE OF ARCHITECTURE
Oslo, Norway
nordicarch.com

Nordic – Office of Architecture is one of Norway's largest architecture firms with offices in Oslo, Copenhagen and Reykjavik, and a staff of 260 architects, interior designers, planners, facade engineers, landscape architects and other specialists. The office shapes buildings, cities and destinations and has designed everything from the world's greenest airport to floating saunas. Nordic's mission is to build a more sustainable society through exceptional architecture that transforms, inspires and enhances the environments in which we live. They specialise in several markets including housing, aviation, culture, healthcare, urban design and commercial development.
page 238

ODAMI
Toronto, Canada
odami.ca

Odami is a Toronto-based design studio offering architectural and interior design services. The studio was founded in 2017 by Spanish architect Aránzazu González Bernardo and Canadian designer Michael Norman Fohring. The studio's focus is to create buildings and spaces that belong: to their place and its story, and to their clients. These parameters present opportunities and characteristics unique to each project. Odami seeks to embody and amplify these qualities through a playful exploration of typology, materiality, craft and light. In this way, each project acquires its own distinct identity; one that fits, and one that lasts.
page 244

PROJECTS OFFICE
London, United Kingdom
projectsoffice.co

Projects Office is a multidisciplinary architecture and design studio based in East London. Their ethos is fantastic pragmatism: thinking laterally, solving problems imaginatively and taking fun seriously. The studio's work combines a joyful aesthetic with serious design quality, rigorous research with a people-centred approach and bold ideas with fine attention to detail. The practice is particularly interested in projects which involve, celebrate, sustain and empower communities, at work, at play or in the city.
page 250

SILO
The Hague, the Netherlands
silo.nl

Silo creates brands and environments that amaze and inspire. Through storytelling, their work connects people to each other and to the values of an organization, strategically aligning identity and the physical environment. Using spatial branding and design, the studio's principal goal is to generate positive impact on the human experience.
page 184

SIVAK+PARTNERS
Odessa, Ukraine
sivak-partners.com

The company was originally founded by Dmitry Sivak in 2015. After three years of rapid growth, Alexey Gulesha and Maksym Iuriichuk joined as new partners. Sivak+Partners currently employs 13 architects and designers and has built projects on several continents. The studio combines business, art and comfort, designing and implementing bold projects from high-rise towers, providing thousands of square metres of workplace, to small cafes serving delicious home-made cookies.
page 188

SIXSEVEN STUDIO
Bangkok, Thailand
sixseven-studio.com

Sixseven Studio is a Bangkok-based design practice founded in 2008 by Pakorn Rattanasuteeranon and Kornkanok Meksilp. The studio provides full architectural and interior design services with their extensive experience in hospitality and retail space. Sixseven Studio focuses on projects nation-wide, from small scale shops to mixed-used projects. With a keen interest in local craft and cultural context, they approach each one differently, believing that each should have its own distinctive character. The practice's team continually explores a new boundary of storytelling in design to ensure not only the practical aspects but a creative way to represent the brand's character is reflected within their design elements.
page 256

SR PROJECTS
New York, USA
srprojects.co

SR Projects is an architecture, interior design and development studio founded in 2019 by Sacha Roubeni whose work ranges from luxury residential, to high-end commercial and spans from local to international. The New York-based office approaches every project as an opportunity to collaborate with its clients in a way that tailors and curates their stories and unique cultures into a livable environment elevated by research, design and the attention to detail on a macro and micro level. Although the aesthetic can vary from space to space, SR Projects applies a consistent underlying focus on materiality, innovation, minimalism, and a touch of the unexpected.
page 54

TUNA
New York, USA
t-u-n-a.com

TUNA is an architecture office established by Christopher Gardner, with projects ranging from small-scale interiors to new multifamily constructions, with an emerging specialisation in retail spaces for the cannabis sector.
page 54

STUDIO KARHARD
Berlin, Germany
karhard.de

studio karhard was founded in 2003 by Thomas Karsten and Alexandra Erhard and currently employs around 9 people. The practice is dedicated to designing indoor environments such as clubs, bars and restaurants as well as medical facilities and retail spaces. Putting themselves in the position of their clients and users allows the architects to acquire extensive knowledge about organization, logistics and requirements for each project. At the same time, using acoustics, light and haptic qualities of space allow the practice to create places where people can act instinctively and feel at ease.
page 58

STUDIOMARSMAN
Delft, the Netherlands
studiomarsman.nl

Founded in 2010, studiomarsman creates spatial designs for private, public and commercial clients. The practice's portfolio ranges from simple refurbishments to large-scale infrastructure projects, from concept to delivery and from scale of an interior to the scale of the city. studiomarsman focuses on quality for the end user, both architecturally, technically and functionally. High-quality simplicity is the result of their structured approach, in which innovative digital tools are often deployed.
page 184

STUDIO PAOLO FERRARI
Toronto, Canada
paoloferrari.com

Studio Paolo Ferrari is a multidisciplinary design studio with a focus on interiors and objects. The studio was founded in 2016 by Paolo Ferrari and has quickly grown into an internationally recognised interior design studio with a global roster of luxury projects. The studio's work emerges through the pursuit of inventive and resonant concepts, led by design strategy, integrity and refinement. The practice's guiding principles are creative thinking, collaboration and optimism, creating design that celebrates the human experience.
page 62

STUDIO PUISTO
Helsinki, Finland
studiopuisto.fi

Studio Puisto is a Helsinki-based boutique architecture studio founded in 2015 by five partners. Today, the 18-strong team designs concepts, builds environments and creates experiences. The practice specialises in hospitality and wellness architecture, with a customer-centric approach. The designs are based on deep understanding of clients' needs, with each solution also tailored to benefit nature and wider society. The studio's embrace of its Nordic roots is reflected in its appreciation for simplicity, authenticity and nature.
page 138

STUDIO RAMOPRIMO
Beijing, China
ramoprimo.com

Studio Ramoprimo is a Beijing-based architectural design practice founded in 2008 by Italian architects Marcella Campa and Stefano Avesani. Studio Ramoprimo's projects range from urban planning to architecture, interior design and graphics. The main focus of the practice is the interaction between the social and the build environment and offering vibrant design solutions at different scales to meet contemporary urban living needs. The studio experiments with materials and thoughts and seeks inspiration behind the challenges that come with every project, the excitement of research, making mistakes, trying again and creating.
page 192

STUDIO REAKTOR
Prague, Czech Republic
studio-reaktor.com

Studio Reaktor prides itself in creating spaces with strong architectural narratives. The work of the practice is based on synergy and interdisciplinary relationships, with new solutions emerging from long-term differences of opinions. Graphic and landscape designers, construction engineers and other specialists essential to providing quality results and development are invited to collaborate during the design process. With unconventional approaches to standard briefs, the practice explores the essence of each project to discover ways of improving the users' environment.
page 196

RO_AR ARCHITECTS
Świnoujście, Poland/
Brno, Czech Republic
ro-ar.eu

Based in both Poland and the Czech Republic, RO_AR Architects was founded by Szymon Rozwałka in 2011. The practice works across both residential and cultural sectors and specialises in designing within existing structures, highlighting the architectural and functional contradictions implicit within the work. According to Rozwałka, this clash of old and new has the potential to trigger unexpected design solutions.
page 132

TAKUYAHOSOKAI
Tokyo, Japan
takuyahosokai.com

TAKUYAHOSOKAI is an architectural studio based in Tokyo, Japan, established by Takuya Hosokai in 2013. The practice operates in the fields of architecture, urbanism and cultural analysis. By conducting meticulous research into global lifestyle, culture, history, economy, religion and politics, the studio aims to create works of architecture as new histories. As old structures in Japan are being lost to development, the studio aims to create a kind of archival architecture, inheriting fragments of the historical cityscape and expressing these memories into the future.
page 200

TEAM55667788
Seoul, South Korea
team55667788.com

TEAM55667788 is an interior design firm founded by Changsung Ryu in 2011 and is known for its unconstrained approach in actualising design concepts while respecting conventional and traditional design philosophies.
page 204

VSHD DESIGN
Dubai, UAE
vshd.net

VSHD Design was founded by interior architect Rania Hamed. The practice aims to transform and re-purpose the space and breathe new life into it, marrying strong concepts with attention to detail. With each project, the architects and designers combine modesty with elegance, beauty and subtle luxury. Hamed is fascinated by the challenge of integrating traditional culture and technique into contemporary design, introducing this dichotomy into the studio's work. VSHD Design has completed both residential and commercial projects across the world.
page 210

WATERFROM DESIGN
Taipei, Taiwan
waterfrom.com

Established in 2008, Waterfrom straddles the fields of interior design and architecture. The practice's guiding principle is that design should be like water, simple and pure, organic and ever-changing, retaining the neatness of water's essence, and displaying possibilities without overbearing conceptual framework. The designers pay special attention to the story and context of the space and time, to create spaces that can convey messages and accommodate emotions. The studio's design director, Nic Lee, has worked in the industry for over a decade, mixing extreme simplicity with humour in his work.
page 260

WIEGERINCK
Arnhem, the Netherlands
wiegerinck.nl

Wiegerinck stands for humane, sustainable and future-proof designs. Founded in 1948, the office mainly works in the field of healthcare, residential care, education and research. Evidence-based design and the Healing Environment concept are fixed pillars for their designs which serve the wellbeing of guests, visitors, patients, clients and employees.
page 68

WUTOPIA LAB
Shanghai, China
wutopialab.com

Wutopia Lab was founded by architect Yu Ting in Shanghai as an architecture company based on a new paradigm of complex systems. The practice uses Shanghai's urban culture and lifestyle as a starting point for all its design, using architecture as a tool to promote sociological progress within building practice. Wutopia Lab focuses on creating human-centric environments and is dedicated to linking different aspects of urban life.
page 144

YASUHIRO SAWA DESIGN OFFICE
Kyoto, Japan
yasuhirosawa.com

Founded in 2014 by Yasuhiro Sawa in Kyoto, Japan, the eponymous practice specialises in commercial interiors, homes and renovations. Taking a fresh approach to each project, the office favours elegant solutions that mediate between spaces, functions and users.
page 216

CREDITS

The Healthy Indoors
New Challenges, New Design

Publisher
Frame

Managing Editor
François-Luc Giraldeau

Editorial Assistant
Heidi Macek

Texts
Peter Smisek

Graphic Design
Zoe Bar-Pereg
Barbara Iwanicka

Prepress
Edward De Nijs

Cover Photography
David Mitchell

Printing
IPP Printers

Trade Distribution USA and Canada
ACC Art Books
6 West 18th Street, Suite 4BNYC, NY 10011
E ussales@accartbooks.com
T +1 212 645 1111
F +1 716 242 4811
Books are billed and shipped
by The National Book Network

Trade Distribution Benelux
Van Ditmar Boekenimport B.V.
Herikerbergweg 98
1101 CM Amsterdam-Zuidoost
the Netherlands
T +31 (0)88-1338473
M +31 (0)6-46205118
vanditmar.nl

Trade Distribution Rest of World
Thames & Hudson Ltd
181A High Holborn
London WC1V 7QX
United Kingdom
T +44 20 7845 5000
F +44 20 7845 5050

ISBN: 978-94-92311-57-3